# To Compose

# To Compose

## Teaching Writing in the High School

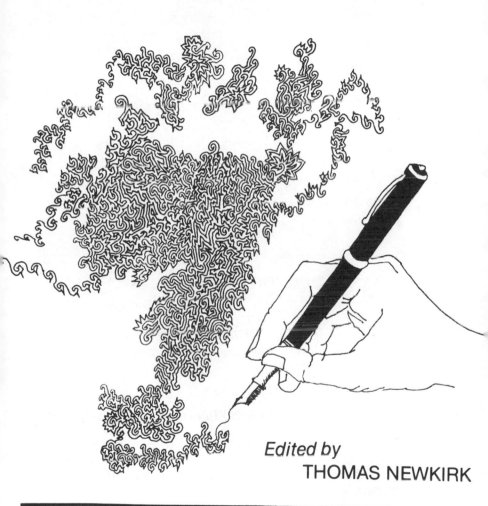

*Edited by*
THOMAS NEWKIRK

**TEACHERS WRITING TO TEACHERS SERIES**

**Heinemann**
**Portsmouth, NH**

**HEINEMANN EDUCATIONAL BOOKS, INC.**
70 Court Street, Portsmouth, NH 03801

London    Edinburgh    Melbourne    Auckland
Hong Kong    Singapore    Kuala Lumpur
New Delhi    Ibadan    Nairobi    Johannesburg
Kingston    Port of Spain

ISBN 0-435-08258-2
Printed and manufactured in the United States of America.
10  9  8  7  6  5  4  3  2  1

# Contents

## WRITING ACROSS THE CURRICULUM

# Introduction

THE *ENGLISH JOURNAL* began publication in 1912, and the lead article in the first issue was entitled: "Can Good Composition Teaching Be Done Under Present Conditions?" It began:

> No.
> This is a small and apparently unprotected word, occupying a somewhat exposed position; but it is upborne by indisputable truth.
> If another answer were possible, if good teaching can be done under present conditions, it is passing strange that so few teachers have found out how to do it; that English composition teachers as a class, if judged by the criticism that is becoming more and more frequent, are so abnormally inefficient. . . . Every year teachers resign, break down, perhaps become permanently invalided, having sacrificed ambition, health, and in not a few instances even life to do all the work expected of them.

In some respects the conditions of the high school teacher have changed little. Classes are too large. Public expectations for education outpace public support. And today reading and writing can seem overly-laborious to students accustomed to a visual medium where problems are always resolved within the hour.

Strange time for a renaissance. But there has been dramatic increase in attention to writing, not simply from those who want to go *back* to basics but from classroom teachers and those in the university who work with classroom teachers. Central to this renewed interest is the rejection of a sterile tradition in composition instruction which emphasized mechanical correctness and prescribed forms — ready-made containers for the student's ideas. This tradition was (and still is) predominantly negative when it came to marking papers; writing was "corrected," the focus on the eradication of error and not on supporting the strengths of the writer. Little wonder that both teachers and students found the writing classroom a joyless place.

But writing instruction began to change in the late 60's and early 70's in large part because teachers and researchers began to ask the right question — what happens when a writer composes? The question has not been (and never will be) answered fully, but it quickly became apparent that the actual processes of practicing writers bore little resemblance to advice of the handbooks. Writers did *not* write to prescribed forms; writers created forms appropriate to the meaning they wanted to convey. Writers often did *not* know exactly where they were going because they had an outline; they regularly talked about making discoveries, of being surprised as they went. Writers often sought out a response from other readers, but they did *not* seek correction. This initial research led inevitably to the question: if we want students to act as writers, shouldn't we treat them as writers?

*To Compose* is a collection of essays which examines the two questions that have rejuvenated composition instruction:

— What does it mean to compose?
— What does it mean to teach composing?

The twelve essays were selected after wide consultation with leading teacher educators in this area. In my letter to them I asked that they nominate articles that have made a difference, that teachers circulate in their schools, that teachers refer to long after any course is done. I asked them to nominate articles that were direct, well-written, serious without being solemn.

From the nominations I selected essays which fell into sections:

1. **Prologue** — Arthur Daigon contrasts traditional instruction in writing with an approach centering around the writing process.

2. **Getting Started** — The poet, William Stafford emphasizes the importance of receptivity in the early stages of composing, a willingness to accept an initial idea or impression and to see where it leads. Donald Murray also looks at the way writers begin, at the signals which tell a writer how and when to begin. Sondra Perl argues that in the act of writing, the writer often has to move backward in order to move forward, and she examines this process which she calls retrospective structuring. William Clark's concluding essay offers practical advice on beginning a program in which students are treated like writers.

3. **Responding to Writing** — Donald Murray explored the first reader who responds to writing — the writer. What kind of reading does a writer do? Linda Flower asks a different question: why are first drafts of writers often difficult to follow. Her essay is a careful examination of the mental processes that produce "writer-based prose," writing not yet crafted for a reader. Stephen Tchudi then describes a classroom where evaluation is not the termination of writing, but is woven into the process of teaching.

4. **Writing and Literature.** Most English classes include both writing and reading — but how are these two most profitably connected? Nancie Atwell argues that the same principles that underly writing instruction should underly reading instruction, and she shows how she united the two in her eighth-grade class. In the other essay in this section, I criticize the traditional form for writing about literature — the critical analysis paper. Both Atwell and I claim that if students are to use writing to make sense of reading, they need to use a less formal more personal language of exploration.

5. **Writing Across the Curriculum.** If writing is a major instrument for learning (and it may be *the* major instrument), it should have a place in all subject areas. But how is writing used in schools? Bryant Fillion reports on a survey which found that *copying* was the most common form of writing in the schools he looked at. Toby Fulwiler shows how teachers in all content areas can use journals where students use expressive language to forge their own meanings.

In addition to the essays themselves I include after each major section a "Time for Questions." Here I pose questions that are regularly asked at workshops, questions like:

1. How can I help students find something to write about?
2. How can I help students become more effective in responding to the papers of their classmates?
3. Is there anything that can be done for high school students with spelling problems?

In some cases I will refer to research in answering these questions, but for the most part I rely on my own experience as a teacher on the high school and college level.

At the end of each section I include a short list of suggested reading. By now the amount of material available about writing is huge, so I have limited the lists to a few books or articles that are both easily available and highly readable.

\*     \*     \*

In putting together this collection I had the help of many people. I want to thank two colleagues, Bob Connors and Thomas Carnicelli for their good advice. I was also fortunate to receive suggestions from Nancie Atwell, Charlie Chew, Ted Hipple, Jane Kearns, Judith Fishman Summerfield, Ann Ruggles Gere, Sally Reagan, Arthur Daigon, Sheila Fitzgerald, James S. Davis, Nancy Wilson, John Mayher, and John Warnock. I'm sure none of these educators will agree fully with my selections, but their recommendations helped me see possibilities I would have otherwise missed.

Again it was good to work with the Northeast Regional Exchange in developing this book. Doug Fleming, as always, was a master at supporting the project and at helping to make it more useful for teachers.

T.N.
Durham, N.H.

# Prologue

# Toward Righting Writing

by ARTHUR DAIGON
*University of Connecticut*

**T**HE BELL RINGS and soon the class settles down, prepared for the writing that Teacher had warned them they would do during this period — and possibly the next. They know the procedure. Last time they compared two characters in a story. Before that they wrote about "An Important Event in My Life," and before that about "Why Marijuana Use Should or Should Not Be Legalized." They wait for today's topic to be written on the board. They wait too for the reminders about complete sentences, about introductory and concluding sentences, about clarity and coherence, about the need for examples and detail, about punctuation and capitalization, and about how an outline will make writing easier. The paper is distributed, and after some perfunctory attempts at outlining they begin to write.

Some 30 minutes later, Teacher suggests that they finish and check their papers for errors — misspelled words, an omitted title, paragraphs that need indenting, and so on. In the time remaining they may begin copying their final drafts, to be handed in tomorrow.

At the next class meeting, Teacher asks them for the assignment. For a variety of reasons, several students have been unable to finish their compositions, but they promise to turn them in, probably the next day. The others hand their completed assignments to Teacher, who expresses the hope that these papers will be better than those written two weeks ago. Teacher then suggests that the class open their grammar texts to the section on correct usage and continue the work interrupted by the composition.

At the end of the day, Teacher brings the papers home, and a few days later begins to grade them. Teacher makes sure that no error is left uncovered. Error-free papers receive higher grades than those with mistakes. Longer, more complex sentences and unusual vocabulary add to the likelihood of a better grade. After several hours *every paper has been corrected and graded. Brief comments accompany the grade at the top of the paper. Sometimes major flaws are noted; sometimes a student is urged to try harder on the next composition. Occasionally, Teacher congratulates a student for an "excellent piece of work."*

*A week has passed and Teacher is ready to return the papers. Once again, the usage exercises are put aside, and Teacher tells the class about several students who misunderstood the assignment, about failure to go beyond generalizations, about lack of support for positions taken, about misspelled words, and about the frequency of run-on sentences.*

*Then Teacher asks several students to read their A-rated papers aloud. These papers will then be displayed on the bulletin board as models of good writing. No one is surprised. These students have read their papers to the class before. After the readings, Teacher returns the compositions, requesting that each correction be noted and each misspelled word be added to the Misspelled Word List kept in each student's notebook. Some students smile; some frown as they consider the grades and the comments on their papers. When the bell rings, they gather their books and move toward the door. Teacher counts four compositions wadded into balls and thrown into the wastebasket — three fewer than the last time.*

In an earlier time, Teacher would be universally commended for a job well done and reassured that the students' failure to improve their writing was to be expected. Teaching composition is a burdensome and frustrating task, but a necessary one. After all, don't teachers need to assign topics? Don't they need to warn students about errors in usage, spelling, punctuation, and the rest? Don't they need to read, correct, and grade everything written by students? Isn't that what they were trained and hired to do? How else are students going to learn to write?

Over the past decade, answers to all of these questions — and more — have filled the pages of the professional journals and dominated the programs at English/language arts conferences. Everyone involved in English/language arts education has been scrambling to transform what research reveals to be the most promising ways to teach composition into workable classroom practices.

Research and the practice of successful writing teachers tell us that virtually every assumption and action of Teacher in the scene above prevents or retards growth in writing competence. From assigning the topic to returning the graded papers, Teacher contradicts what we have come to know about how writing happens — or should happen — in school and out.

Writing specialists agree that writing is an immensely complex process. To produce a successful composition, a writer must find out what to say about a subject and how to arrange the saying. A writer must adjust the subject and the saying to the purpose of the writing, to the intended audience, and to his or her own rhetorical stance toward all of these. A writer must accommodate the conventions of his or her chosen mode of composition and the linguistic etiquette expected of those who write English.

These discoveries, arrangements, and accommodations that produce good writing are achieved through the performance of an intricate and demanding ritual — a continuous cycle of exploration, rehearsal, drafting, and revision that leads to new exploration, rehearsal, drafting, and revision. Attention to the demands of the composing process and to what teachers and peers can do to make it work is at the center of a revolution in the way writing is perceived and taught. The traditional pedagogy of *select the topic, correct the error,* and *expect improvement* is still widely practiced. But — given the failures of the old writing regime, the ardor of the insurgents, and the success of the reforms they propose — not for long.

Nearly all reservations about Teacher's way of teaching and the alternatives to it derive from the work of composition researchers and teachers known by their peers as major contributors to our knowledge about writing. The research of James Britton, Janet Emig, Donald Graves, and Sondra Perl and the commentary of Stephen Tchudi, James Moffett, and Donald Murray are essential to understanding the composing process and its application in the public schools.

## The Assignment

*The bell rings and soon the class settles down, prepared for the writing that Teacher had warned them they would do during this period — and possibly the next. They know the procedure. Last time they compared two characters in a story. Before that they wrote about "An Important Event in My Life," and before that about "Why Marijuana Use Should or Should Not Be Legalized." They wait for today's topic to be written on the board.*

Teacher's assignment comes out of the blue, disconnected from any earlier event that might justify writing. Today is composition day on Teacher's schedule, and that, rather than any experience — personal or public, real or fictional, pragmatic or expressive — determines what students will be doing that afternoon. No case is made to or solicited from students for the topics presented to the class. Occasionally and for a special reason, a teacher might justifiably assign a topic "cold," but most writing assignments should progress logically from some earlier engagement.

Whatever the earlier engagement, the assignment should indicate the purpose of the writing, the intended audience, and the stance of the writer. This applies to writing that emphasizes personal experience as well as to more objective exposition. Consider two examples: Having created a small community store, a class of second-graders was asked to write to candy companies requesting stock — a writing situation that proceeds logically from an earlier event with clearly defined rhetorical circumstances. A 12th-grade class was asked to assume the role of a minor character in *Hamlet* and in a letter to the king assess Hamlet's behavior and its likely consequences. Here again, the assignment springs from an earlier encounter — an encounter with a literary text — and the assignment defines the purpose, the audience, and the voice of the writer.

### Pre-Writing

*They wait too for the reminders about complete sentences, about introductory and concluding sentences, about clarity and coherence, about the need for examples and detail, about punctuation and capitalization, and about how an outline will make writing easier. The paper is distributed, and after some perfunctory attempts at outlining they begin to write.*

Teacher's routine reminders about linguistic and structural lapses can only distract students from more urgent claims on their attention. They need to consider the requirements of the assignment, to recall relevant experiences, and to connect them with their understanding of the task. They must determine the voice or tone that best suits the audience and purposes and consider the framework that might best hold the composition together. Finally, they need to rehearse all of these elements, singly and in combination, for the inner director who can "listen," judge, and help reshape each possibility. Reluctance to begin the physical act of writing may well be the inner director's signal that more exploration, planning, and rehearsal are necessary.

The teacher can help by providing time and suggesting ways to activate these processes before the pen touches paper. Discussing the subject, brainstorming, exchanging parallel experiences, role playing, referring to similar or contrasting events in the media — all of these help to generate and shape substance, to clarify rhetorical circumstances, and to suggest structural possibilities. To determine what comes first and what follows rarely requires a formal outline — a pre-writing device that discourages the composing process and is ignored by most successful writers.

All of this tentative invention and organization is subject to the changes demanded by the internal director during the countless rehearsals that take place from pre-writing up to the moment that the paper, finally completed, leaves the writer's hands. Only after the pre-writing activities have done their work and after the changes demanded by the inner director have been made and rehearsed does a writer set down that first reluctant string of words. And these are but the beginning of a first draft.

The cognitive foreplay of pre-writing is essential to the writing act. Teachers need to provide time for it in their composition classes.

## Drafting

*Some 30 minutes later, Teacher suggests that they finish and check their papers for errors — misspelled words, an omitted title, paragraphs that need indenting, and so on. In the time remaining they may begin copying their final drafts, to be handed in tomorrow.*

Teacher's warnings about various linguistic oversights are ill-timed. No one would presume to interrupt a playwright and a director as they sketch performance strategies with the leading actors. Decisions about seating arrangements, background music in the second act, and the color of the leading lady's costume would be set aside for a later time.

In the same way, details better attended to later should not be allowed to stymie the performance of the first draft of a composition. To burden a writer struggling over issues of substance and form with violations of linguistic etiquette can only retard or block altogether the flow of language onto paper. To encourage this flow, many teachers recommend "free writing" — a technique in which a writer sets down the words, phrases, and sentences suggested by a topic in a continuous stream, uninterrupted by attention to mechanical or grammatical blunders. Because the mind is focused on retrieving ideas and feelings and converts them almost automatically into language, the stream of words can be maintained. Finding and correcting errors at this critical time would squander a writer's planning and decision-making resources. Spelling, punctuation, capitalization, appropriate usage, and complete sentences *are* important and must be attended to. But this can be done more efficiently in a later draft.

Teacher assumed that students needed only 30 minutes to discover and shape their compositions and a few more minutes to "check their papers." That left only the final copying to be done. Too frequently this produces only a neater version of a first draft, shorn of a few of the grosser errors.

To grasp the near impossibility of composing without frequent opportunities to draft, revise, and draft again, Teacher need only try the assignment along with the students. The experience should persuade Teacher to provide time for these essential elements of composing.

### Revising

Except for a virtually useless suggestion to check for errors, Teacher had made no provision for revising — a process many writers consider the *real* task of writing. Just as a play director deals with weaknesses revealed during the first run-through of a play, so must a writer respond to a first draft. Some words and sentences do not work on paper as anticipated. The argument that seemed so clearcut when first approved by the inner director appears ragged on the page. The tone seems not exactly right for the intended audience. The opening sentence is vague and wordy and will need reworking. A word or a phrase suggests another line of inquiry that ought to be pursued. The transition between the second and third paragraphs is flawed. Too many embedded relative clauses cloud the last section. A new and more convincing resolution of the argument needs to be invented.

Revision, not to be confused with proofreading, is the effort to reconcile the scheme provisionally approved by the inner director with what has materialized as the first draft. A writer may find that the first draft omits or distorts elements in the original plan and thus requires structural revision. On the other hand, there may be unanticipated strengths in the first draft that should be retained and elaborated, thus requiring changes in the original concept. During revision, both draft and concept are modified through a recurring, overlapping, fugue-like process called into play during earlier writing stages. Words, sentences, and paragraphs undergo continuous rehearsal and revision — the one process blending into and becoming indistinguishable from the other. Not only the draft, but the plan, the rhetorical relationships, and, most interesting of all, the writer's understanding of the subject undergo the process of rehearsal and revision. Frequently, writers change their minds as well as their texts.

All of this may seem to apply only to accomplished writers. Can students find what has to be modified in a draft? Can they make the changes that will add cogency and clarity to their writing? Are their inner directors capable of passing informed judgment on suggested rearrangements?

Because students are least experienced and comfortable with revision, they need more help with this than with other phases of the composing process. They are generally unfamiliar with matters of adding, cutting, and rearrangement and must be taught. A critical audience recruited from outside the classroom offers the strongest incentive to learn. In the traditional role of grader, however, the teacher has proved ineffectual. Suggestions written on papers completed the previous week exert little influence on how students handle revision problems that surface during the next composing performance.

To improve students' revision, teachers will have to change from graders looking for improvement next time to working editors responding to drafts in progress. In their new role teachers will collect drafts and — at home, on hall duty, or in class — will scribble reactions, questions, and suggestions about subjects and their treatment. They will take time in class to work on common problems found in several of the drafts. They will conduct brief conferences with individual students while others are redrafting or meeting in groups. At other times teachers will circulate, looking over shoulders, asking questions, recommending changes. Sometimes whole compositions or excerpts will be read aloud or flashed on a screen or written on the board to give students practice discussing specific writing problems and their solutions.

Yet, if teachers are to survive the demands of a workshop setting, they will have to enlist the aid of other surrogate inner directors who can help with revision. Groups of three or four students can provide useful feedback about whether a piece of writing is working, where its strengths and weaknesses lie, and what can be done to make it better. This is likely to happen when a teacher initially suggests specific questions to be asked or elements to be considered. It is likely to happen when students are encouraged to respond as the intended audience would. It is likely to happen when students see their teacher as an editor and learn to ask similar questions and recommend similar remedies.

As a piece of writing approaches completion, proofreading becomes more important. The teacher may give lessons on proofreading problems common to the class. Students may become specialists in spelling or punctuation or capitalization and put their skills at the disposal of the class. The composition/grammar text is now useful as students consult it for correct usages and formats. Students may meet in groups to monitor one another's papers and recommend still more redrafting.

As students gain confidence and ability to conduct rehearsals and recommend revisions in drafts written by their peers, these new directing skills can be applied to their own drafts as well. This signifies the birth of an informed inner director capable of listening and judging.

## Publication

*Then Teacher asks several students to read their A-rated papers aloud. These papers will then be displayed on the bulletin board as models of good writing. No one is surprised. These students have read their papers to the class before.*

Publication provides an audience for writing; it transforms a required exercise into a purposeful activity and stiff, flat prose into lively discourse. Having an audience other than a grade-dispensing teacher can act as a powerful incentive to work hard at writing well.

For the few with A-rated papers, Teacher provided a captive audience of students. Teacher intended these papers to be taken as models of good writing. For the student audience, however, these papers only confirmed what they have come to believe are their own inadequacies. Teacher could have involved other students by publishing, if not whole compositions, at least successful paragraphs or even sentences.

In classes where students draft, revise, and draft again until the best possible paper emerges, the teacher posts papers on bulletin boards and collects them in booklets for circulation throughout the school and the community. In such classes, what students write about their school, their community, their country is made available to appropriate readers — the principal, the mayor, the manager of the television station, the newspaper editor, the local legislator. Book reports are aimed at and delivered to other classes. Invitations, catalog orders, tourist information, and consumer complaints are directed to appropriate readers. When writers write for a specific audience, they internalize that audience and consult it as they write. In effect, the writer's conception of an audience acts as a visiting inner director.

Publication need not depend entirely on real audiences. For example, students may write advice, criticism, and commentary to the people they meet in fairy tales, myths, short stories, and novels. Because such messages cannot be delivered to the intended audience, other students can assume an appropriate role and write logical replies. To do this, student writers need knowledge of a character's situation, and thus they must engage in a closer reading of the story. This technique is a good way to connect writing to another part of the English/language arts curriculum.

## Evaluation

*Teacher brings the papers home, and a few days later begins to grade them. Teacher makes sure that no error is left uncorrected. Error-free papers receive higher grades than those with mistakes. Longer, more complex sentences and unusual vocabulary add to the likelihood of a better grade. After several hours every paper has been corrected and graded. Brief comments accompany the grade at the top of the paper. . . .*

*A week has passed, and Teacher is ready to return the papers. . . . Teacher tells the class about several students who misunderstood the assignment, about failure to go beyond generalizations, about lack of support for positions taken, about misspelled words, and about the frequency of run-on sentences. . . . Teacher returns the compositions, requesting that each correction be noted and each misspelled word be added to the Misspelled Word List kept in each student's notebook. Some students smile; some frown as they consider the grades and comments on their papers. When the bell rings, they gather their books and move toward the door. Teacher counts four compositions wadded into balls and thrown into the wastebasket — three fewer than the last time.*

For Teacher, evaluation means correcting and tallying errors and assigning a grade. Although such practices have been shown to produce no noticeable improvement in subsequent writing, Teacher is committed to correcting and grading everything put on paper. Teacher views all writing performances as final performances whose flaws must be noted and reckoned in a grade.

Teacher's colleague, the football coach, expects blunders from his players. He knows that practice sessions will work out the problems and turn rookies into competent performers. He does not penalize players during practice sessions (nor, for that matter, during games). He supplies concrete suggestions about how to improve passing, running, or blocking skills and makes time to work out problems — alone and with the team. Teacher would do well to consider such a model of instruction and evaluation.

A grade is a crude device to apply to the complex phenomenon that is a composition. What does a grade tell a writer about his or her writing? About invention? Organization? A sense of audience? Coherence? Clarity? Tone? Syntactic fluency? Usage, mechanics, spelling, handwriting? Which are most important? Do we presume to judge all composition traits with one grade? Two? Do we assign a separate grade for each? Should a grade report "achievement" or "progress" in a student's writing? Does the grade report competence relative to other writers in the class, in the district, in the state? Or does it report "absolute" competence? How reliable are grades anyway?

These questions and the reservations they imply have convinced many who teach composition that grading drains their time and energies without contributing either to improved writing or to accurate assessment of writing performance. Despite this widespread disaffection with grading, composition teachers — under pressure from parents, students, and administrators — will undoubtedly continue to defuse the worst misunderstandings that inevitably plague those who grade and those who are graded by adopting these alternatives to conventional grading:

• Keep a folder of each student's writing — including drafts and revisions. Inside the folder students record the nature of the writing task, the dates it was undertaken and completed, and comments by peers and by you about weaknesses to be addressed, strengths to be maintained, and relapses suffered. Periodic review of the folder can focus on progress made and progress still needed, rather than on the pattern of letter grades.

• Meet with each student in a brief conference and focus on particular elements crucial to the success of an assignment. A checklist of such primary traits takes the place of a letter grade and becomes the occasion for revision.

• Midway through a semester and again at its end, allow students to choose two or three pieces of writing to be graded. Thus the grades will reflect the best the students can do. Encourage students to grade these papers and to compare their grades and how they were determined with yours and how you arrived at them.

• Try open-ended grading. Encourage students to revise and rewrite a composition and possibly earn a higher grade.

## Epilogue

*Teacher's light is still burning. The stack of compositions, begun nearly two hours earlier, is dwindling. Teacher's red pencil has found its quota of errors and oversights and has duly recorded the consequences in a black grade book. After the last author has been urged to try harder and a grade assigned, Teacher sits back, weary but pleased with a difficult job thoroughly done, and murmurs, "They'll probably do better next time."*

## Selected Bibliography

Britton, James, et al. *The Development of Writing Ability, 11-18.* London: Macmillan, 1975.

Emig, Janet. *The Composing Process of Twelfth-Graders.* Urbana, Ill.: National Council of Teachers of English, 1971.

Graves, Donald. "A New Look at Research in Writing," in Shirley Haley-James, ed., *Perspectives on Writing in Grades 1-8.* Urbana, Ill.: National Council of Teachers of English, 1981.

Judy, Stephen. *Explorations in the Teaching of English.* New York: Harper & Row, 1981.

Moffett, James. *Teaching the Universe of Discourse.* Boston: Houghton Mifflin, 1968.

_____ and Betty Jane Wagner. *Student-Centered Language Arts and Reading, K-13.* Boston: Houghton Mifflin, 1976.

Murray, Donald M. *A Writer Teaches Writing.* Boston: Houghton Mifflin, 1968.

_____. "Writing Process: How Writing Finds Its Own Meaning," in Timothy R. Donovan and Ben W. McClelland, eds., *Eight Approaches to Teaching Composition.* Urbana, Ill.: National Council of Teachers of English, 1980.

Perl, Sondra. "The Composing Processes of Unskilled College Writers." *Research in the Teaching of English,* vol. 13, 1979, pp. 363-69.

# Getting Started

# A Way of Writing

by WILLIAM STAFFORD

A WRITER IS NOT so much someone who has something to say as he is someone who has found a process that will bring about new things he would not have thought of if he had not started to say them. That is, he does not draw on a reservoir; instead, he engages in an activity that brings to him a whole succession of unforeseen stories, poems, essays, plays, laws, philosophies, religions, or — but wait!

Back in school, from the first when I began to try to write things, I felt this richness. One thing would lead to another; the world would give and give. Now, after twenty years or so of trying, I live by that certain richness, an idea hard to pin, difficult to say, and perhaps offensive to some. For there are strange implications in it.

One implication is the importance of just plain receptivity. When I write, I like to have an interval before me when I am not likely to be interrupted. For me, this means usually the early morning, before others are awake. I get pen and paper, take a glance out the window (often it is dark out there), and wait. It is like fishing. But I do not wait very long, for there is always a nibble — and this is where receptivity comes in. To get started I will accept anything that occurs to me. Something always occurs, of course, to any of us. We can't keep from thinking. Maybe I have to settle for an immediate impression: it's cold, or hot, or dark, or bright, or in between! Or — well, the possibilities are endless. If I put down something, that thing will help the next thing come, and I'm off. If I let the process go on, things will occur to me that were not at all in my mind when I started. These things, odd or trivial as they may be, are somehow connected. And if I let them string out, surprising things will happen.

If I let them string out. . . . Along with initial receptivity, then, there is another readiness: I must be willing to fail. If I am to keep on writing, I cannot bother to insist on high standards. I must get into action and not let anything stop me, or even slow me much. By "standards" I do not mean "correctness" — spelling, punctuation, and so on. These details become mechanical for anyone who writes for a while. I am thinking about what many people would consider "important" standards, such matters as social significance, positive values, consistency, etc. I resolutely disregard these. Something better, greater, is happening! I am following a process that leads so wildly and originally into new territory that no judgment can at the moment be made about values, significance, and so on. I am making something new, something that has not been judged before. Later others — and maybe I myself — will make judgments. Now, I am headlong to discover. Any distraction may harm the creating.

So, receptive, careless of failure, I spin out things on the page. And a wonderful freedom comes. If something occurs to me, it is all right to accept it. It has one justification: it occurs to me. No one else can guide me. I must follow my own weak, wandering, diffident impulses.

A strange bonus happens. At times, without my insisting on it, my writings become coherent; the successive elements that occur to me are clearly related. They lead by themselves to new connections. Sometimes the language, even the syllables that happen along, may start a trend. Sometimes the materials alert me to something waiting in my mind, ready for sustained attention. At such times, I allow myself to be eloquent, or intentional, or for great swoops (treacherous! not to be trusted!) reasonable. But I do not insist on any of that, for I know that back of my activity there will be the coherence of my self, and that indulgence of my impulses will bring recurrent patterns and meanings again.

This attitude toward the process of writing creatively suggests a problem for me, in terms of what others say. They talk about "skills" in writing. Without denying that I do have experience, wide reading, automatic orthodoxies and maneuvers of various kinds, I still must insist that I am often baffled about what "skill" has to do with the precious little area of confusion when I do not know what I am going to say and then I find out what I am going to say. That precious interval I am unable to bridge by skill. What can I witness about it? It remains mysterious, just as all of us must feel puzzled about how we are so inventive as to be able to talk along through complexities with our friends, not needing to plan what we are going to say, but never stalled for long in our confident forward progress. Skill? If so, it is the skill we all have, something we must have learned before the age of three or four.

A writer is one who has become accustomed to trusting that grace, or luck, or — skill.

Yet another attitude I find necessary: most of what I write, like most of what I say in casual conversation, will not amount to much. Even I will realize, and even at the time, that it is not negotiable. It will be like practice. In conversation I allow myself random remarks — in fact, as I recall, that is the way I learned to talk — so in writing I launch many expendable efforts. A result of this free way of writing is that I am not writing for others, mostly; they will not see the product at all unless the activity eventuates in something that later appears to be worthy. My guide is the self, and its adventuring in the language brings about communication.

This process-rather-than-substance view of writing invites a final, dual reflection:

1) Writers may not be special — sensitive or talented in any usual sense. They are simply engaged in sustained use of a language skill we all have. Their "creations" come about through confident reliance on stray impulses that will, with trust, find occasional patterns that are satisfying.

2) But writing itself is one of the great, free human activities. There is scope for individuality, and elation, and discovery, in writing. For the person who follows with trust and forgiveness what occurs to him, the world remains always ready and deep, an inexhaustible environment, with the combined vividness of an actuality and flexibility of a dream. Working back and forth between experience and thought, writers have more than space and time can offer. They have the whole unexplored realm of human vision.

# Understanding Composing

by SONDRA PERL
*Herbert Lehman College*
*City University of New York*

> Any psychological process, whether the development of thought or voluntary behavior, is a process undergoing changes right before one's eyes. . . . Under certain conditions it becomes possible to trace this development!
>
> L. S. Vygotsky

> It's hard to begin this case study of myself as a writer because even as I'm searching for a beginning, a pattern of organization, I'm watching myself, trying to understand my behavior. As I sit here in silence, I can see lots of things happening that never made it onto my tapes. My mind leaps from the task at hand to what I need at the vegetable stand for tonight's soup to the threatening rain outside to ideas voiced in my writing group this morning, but in between "distractions" I hear myself trying out words I might use. It's as if the extraneous thoughts are a counterpoint to the more steady attention I'm giving to composing. This is all to point out that the process is more complex than I'm aware of, but I think my tapes reveal certain basic patterns that I tend to follow.
>
> Anne
> New York City Teacher

ANNE IS A TEACHER of writing. In 1979, she was among a group of twenty teachers who were taking a course in research and basic writing at New York University[2] One of the assignments in the course was for the teachers to tape their thoughts while composing aloud on the topic, "My Most Anxious Moment as a Writer." Everyone in the group was given the topic in the morning during class and told to compose later on that day in a place where they would be comfortable and relatively free from distractions. The result was a tape of composing aloud and a written product that formed the basis for class discussion over the next few days.

One of the purposes of this assignment was to provide teachers with an opportunity to see their own composing processes at work. From the start of the course, we recognized that we were controlling the situation by assigning a topic and that we might be altering the process by asking writers to compose aloud. Nonetheless we viewed the task as a way of capturing some of the flow of composing and, as Anne later observed in her analysis of her tape, she was able to detect certain basic patterns. This observation, made not only by Anne, then leads me to ask "What basic patterns seem to occur during composing?" and "What does this type of research have to tell us about the nature of the composing process?"

Perhaps the most challenging part of the answer is the recognition of recursiveness in writing. In recent years, many researchers including myself have questioned the traditional notion that writing is a linear process with a strict plan-write-revise sequence? In its stead, we have advocated the idea that writing is a recursive process, that throughout the process of writing, writers return to substrands of the overall process, or subroutines (short successions of steps that yield results on which the writer draws in taking the next set of steps); writers use these to keep the process moving forward. In other words, recursiveness in writing implies that there is a forward-moving action that exists by virtue of a backward-moving action. The questions that then need to be answered are, "To what do writers move back?" "What exactly is being repeated?" "What recurs?"

To answer these questions, it is important to look at what writers do while writing and what an analysis of their processes reveals. The descriptions that follow are based on my own observations of the composing processes of many types of writers including college students, graduate students, and English teachers like Anne.

Writing does appear to be recursive, yet the parts that recur seem to vary from writer to writer and from topic to topic. Furthermore, some recursive elements are easy to spot while others are not.

1) The most visible recurring feature or backward movement involves re-reading little bits of discourse. Few writers I have seen write for long periods of time without returning briefly to what is already down on the page.

For some, like Anne, rereading occurs after every few phrases; for others, it occurs after every sentence; more frequently, it occurs after a "chunk" of information has been written. Thus, the unit that is reread is not necessarily a syntactic one, but rather a semantic one as defined by the writer.

2) The second recurring feature is some key word or item called up by the topic. Writers consistently return to their notion of the topic throughout the process of writing. Particularly when they are stuck, writers seem to use the topic or a key word in it as a way to get going again. Thus many times it is possible to see writers "going back," rereading the topic they were given, changing it to suit what they have been writing or changing what they have written to suit their notion of the topic.

3) There is also a third backward movement in writing, one that is not so easy to document. It is not easy because the move, itself, cannot immediately be identified with words. In fact, the move is not to any words on the page nor to the topic but to feelings or non-verbalized perceptions that *surround* the words, or to what the words already present *evoke* in the writer. The move draws on sense experience, and it can be observed if one pays close attention to what happens when writers pause and seem to listen or otherwise react to what is inside of them. The move occurs inside the writer, to what is physically felt. The term used to describe this focus of writers' attention is *felt sense*. The term "felt sense" has been coined and described by Eugene Gendlin, a philosopher at the University of Chicago. In his words, felt sense is

> the soft underbelly of thought . . . a kind of bodily awareness that . . . can be used as a tool . . . a bodily awareness that . . . encompasses everything you feel and know about a given subject at a given time. . . . It is felt in the body, yet it has meanings. It is body *and* mind before they are split apart.[1]

This felt sense is always there, within us. It is unifying, and yet, when we bring words to it, it can break apart, shift, unravel, and become something else. Gendlin has spent many years showing people how to work with their felt sense. Here I am making connections between what he has done and what I have seen happen as people write.

When writers are given a topic, the topic itself evokes a felt sense in them. This topic calls forth images, words, ideas, and vague fuzzy feelings that are anchored in the writer's body. What is elicited, then, is not solely the product of a mind but of a mind alive in a living, sensing body.

When writers pause, when they go back and repeat key words, what they seem to be doing is waiting, paying attention to what is still vague and unclear. They are looking to their felt experience, and waiting for an image, a word, or a phrase to emerge that captures the sense they embody.

Usually, when they make the decision to write, it is after they have a dawning awareness that something has clicked, that they have enough of a sense that if they begin with a few words heading in a certain direction, words will continue to come which will allow them to flesh out the sense they have.

The process of using what is sensed directly about a topic is a natural one. Many writers do it without any conscious awareness that that is what they are doing. For example, Anne repeats the words "anxious moments," using these key words as a way of allowing her sense of the topic to deepen. She asks herself, "Why are exams so anxiety provoking?" and waits until she has enough of a sense within her that she can go in a certain direction. She does not yet have the words, only the sense that she is able to begin. Once she writes, she stops to see what is there. She maintains a highly recursive composing style throughout and she seems unable to go forward without first going back to see and to listen to what she has already created. In her own words, she says:

> My disjointed style of composing is very striking to me. I almost never move from the writing of one sentence directly to the next. After each sentence I pause to read what I've written, assess, sometimes edit and think about what will come next. I often have to read the several preceding sentences a few times as if to gain momentum to carry me to the next sentence. I seem to depend a lot on the sound of my words and . . . while I'm hanging in the middle of this uncompleted thought, I may also start editing a previous sentence or get an inspiration for something which I want to include later in the paper.

What tells Anne that she is ready to write? What is the feeling of "momentum" like for her? What is she hearing as she listens to the "sound" of her words? When she experiences "inspiration," how does she recognize it?

In the approach I am presenting, the ability to recognize what one needs to do or where one needs to go is informed by calling on felt sense. This is the internal criterion writers seem to use to guide them when they are planning, drafting, and revising.

The recursive move, then, that is hardest to document but is probably the most important to be aware of is the move to felt sense, to what is not yet *in words* but out of which images, words, and concepts emerge.

The continuing presence of this felt sense, waiting for us to discover it and see where it leads, raises a number of questions.

Is "felt sense" another term for what professional writers call their "inner voice" or their feeling of "inspiration"?

Do skilled writers call on their capacity to sense more readily than unskilled writers?

Rather than merely reducing the complex act of writing to a neat formulation, can the term "felt sense" point us to an area of our experience from which we can evolve even richer and more accurate descriptions of composing?

Can learning how to work with felt sense teach us about creativity and release us from stultifyingly repetitive patterns?

My observations lead me to answer "yes" to all four questions. There seems to be a basic step in the process of it and that less skilled writers rely on even when they are unaware of it and that less skilled writers can be taught. This process seems to rely on very careful attention to one's inner reflections and is often accompanied with bodily sensations.

When it's working, this process allows us to say or write what we've never said before, to create something new and fresh, and occasionally it provides us with the experience of "newness" or "freshness," even when "old words" or images are used.

The basic process begins with paying attention. If we are given a topic, it begins with taking the topic in and attending to what it evokes in us. There is less "figuring out" an answer and more "waiting" to see what forms. Even without a predetermined topic, the process remains the same. We can ask ourselves, "What's on my mind?" or "Of all the things I know about, what would I most like to write about now?" and wait to see what comes. What we pay attention to is the part of our bodies where we experience ourselves directly. For many people, it's the area of their stomachs; for others, there is a more generalized response and they maintain a hovering attention to what they experience throughout their bodies.

Once a felt sense forms, we match words to it. As we begin to describe it, we get to see what is there for us. We get to see what we think, what we know. If we are writing about something that truly interests us, the felt sense deepens. We know that we are writing out of a "centered" place.

If the process is working, we begin to move along, sometimes quickly. Other times, we need to return to the beginning, to reread, to see if we captured what we meant to say. Sometimes after rereading we move on again, picking up speed. Other times by rereading we realize we've gone off the track, that what we've written doesn't quite "say it," and we need to reassess. Sometimes the words are wrong and we need to change them. Other times we need to go back to the topic, to call up the sense it initially evoked to see where and how our words led us astray. Sometimes in rereading we discover that the topic is "wrong," that the direction we discovered in writing is where we really want to go. It is important here to clarify that the terms "right" and "wrong" are not necessarily meant to refer to grammatical structures or to correctness.

What is "right" or "wrong" corresponds to our sense of our intention. We intend to write something, words come, and now we assess if those words adequately capture our intended meaning. Thus, the first question we ask ourselves is "Are these words right for me?" "Do they capture what I'm trying to say?" "If not, what's missing?"

Once we ask "what's missing?" we need once again to wait, to let a felt sense of what is missing form, and then to write out of that sense.

I have labeled this process of attending, of calling up a felt sense, and of writing out of that place, the process of *retrospective structuring*. It is retrospective in that it begins with what is already there, inchoately, and brings whatever is there forward by using language in structured form.

It seems as though a felt sense has within it many possible structures or forms. As we shape what we intend to say, we are further structuring our sense while correspondingly shaping our piece of writing.

It is also important to note that what is there implicitly, without words, is not equivalent to what finally emerges. In the process of writing, we begin with what is inchoate and end with something that is tangible. In order to do so, we both discover and construct what we mean. Yet the term "discovery" ought not lead us to think that meaning exists fully formed inside of us and that all we need do is dig deep enough to release it. In writing, meaning cannot be discovered the way we discover an object on an archeological dig. In writing, meaning is crafted and constructed. It involves us in a process of coming-into-being. Once we have worked at shaping, through language, what is there inchoately, we can look at what we have written to see if it adequately captures what we intended. Often at this moment discovery occurs. We see something new in our writing that comes upon us as a surprise. We see in our words a further structuring of the sense we began with and we recognize that in those words we have discovered something new about ourselves and our topic. Thus when we are successful at this process, we end up with a product that teaches us something, that clarifies what we know (or what we knew at one point only implicitly), and that lifts out or explicates or enlarges our experience. In this way, writing leads to discovery.

All the writers I have observed, skilled and unskilled alike, use the process of retrospective structuring while writing. Yet the degree to which they do so varies and seems, in fact, to depend upon the model of the writing process that they have internalized. Those who realize that writing can be a recursive process have an easier time with waiting, looking, and discovering. Those who subscribe to the linear model find themselves easily frustrated when what they write does not immediately correspond to what they planned or when what they produce leaves them with little sense of accomplishment. Since they have relied on a formulaic approach, they often produce writing that is formulaic as well, thereby cutting themselves off from the possibility of discovering something new.

Such a result seems linked to another feature of the composing process, to what I call *projective structuring*, or the ability to craft what one intends to say so that it is intelligible to others.

A number of concerns arise in regard to projective structuring; I will mention only a few that have been raised for me as I have watched different writers at work.

1) Although projective structuring is only one important part of the composing process, many writers act as if it is the whole process. These writers focus on what they think others want them to write rather than looking to see what it is they want to write. As a result, they often ignore their felt sense and they do not establish a living connection between themselves and their topic.

2) Many writers reduce projective structuring to a series of rules or criteria for evaluating finished discourse. These writers ask, "Is what I'm writing correct?" and "Does it conform to the rules I've been taught?" While these concerns are important, they often overshadow all others and lock the writer in the position of writing solely or primarily for the approval of readers.

Projective structuring, as I see it, involves much more than imagining a strict audience and maintaining a strict focus on correctness. It is true that to handle this part of the process well, writers need to know certain grammatical rules and evaluative criteria, but they also need to know how to call up a sense of their reader's needs and expectations.

For projective structuring to function fully, writers need to draw on their capacity to move away from their own words, to decenter from the page, and to project themselves into the role of the reader. In other words, projective structuring asks writers to attempt to become readers and to imagine what someone other than themselves will need before the writer's particular piece of writing can become intelligible and compelling. To do so, writers must have the experience of being readers. They cannot call up a felt sense of a reader unless they themselves have experience what it means to be lost in a piece of writing or to be excited by it. When writers do not have such experiences, it is easy for them to accept that readers merely require correctness.

In closing, I would like to suggest that retrospective and projective structuring are two parts of the same basic process. Together they form the alternating mental postures writers assume as they move through the act of composing. The former relies on the ability to go inside, to attend to what is there, from that attending to place words upon a page, and then to assess if those words adequately capture one's meaning. The latter relies on the ability to assess how the words on that page will affect someone other than the writer, the reader. We rarely do one without the other entering in; in fact, again in these postures we can see the shuttling back-and-forth movements of the composing process, the move from sense to words and from words to sense, from inner experience to outer judgment and from judgment back to experience. As we move through this cycle, we are continually composing and recomposing our meanings and what we mean. And in doing so, we display some of the basic recursive patterns that writers who observe themselves closely seem to see in their own work. After observing the process for a long time we may, like Anne, conclude that at any given moment the process is more complex than anything we are aware of; yet such insights, I believe, are important. They show us the fallacy of reducing the composing process to a simple linear scheme and they leave us with the potential for creating even more powerful ways of understanding composing.

## Notes:

1. L. S. Vygotsky, *Mind in Society*, trans. M. Cole, V. John-Steiner, S. Scribner, and E. Souberman (Cambridge, Mass.: Harvard University Press, 1978), p. 61.

2. This course was team-taught by myself and Gordon Pradl, Associate Professor of English Education at New York University.

3. See Janet Emig, *The Composing Processes of Twelfth-Graders*, NCTE Research Report No. 13 (Urbana, Ill.: National Council of Teachers of English, 1971); Linda Flower and J. R. Hayes, "The Cognition of Discovery," CCC, 31 (February, 1980), 21-32; Nancy Sommers, "The Need for Theory in Composition Research," CCC, 30 (February, 1979), 46-49.

4. Eugene Gendlin, *Focusing* (New York: Everest House, 1978), pp. 35, 165.

# Write Before Writing

by DONALD MURRAY
*University of New Hampshire*

W E COMMAND OUR students to write and grow frustrated when our "bad" students hesitate, stare out the window, dawdle over blank paper, give up and say, "I can't write," while the "good" students smugly pass their papers in before the end of the period.

When publishing writers visit such classrooms, however, they are astonished at students who can write on command, ejaculating correct little essays without thought, for writers have to write before writing.

The writers were the students who dawdled, stared out windows, and, more often than we like to admit, didn't do well in English — or in school.

One reason may be that few teachers have ever allowed adequate time for prewriting, that essential stage in the writing process which precedes a completed first draft. And even the curricula plans and textbooks which attempt to deal with prewriting usually pass over it rather quickly referring only to the techniques of outlining, note-taking, or journal-making, not revealing the complicated process writers work through to get to the first draft.

Writing teachers, however, should give careful attention to what happens between the moment the writer receives an idea or an assignment and the moment the first completed draft is begun. We need to understand, as well as we can, the complicated and intertwining processes of perception and conception through language.

In actual practice, of course, these stages overlap and interact with one another, but to understand what goes on we must separate them and look at them artificially, the way we break down any skill to study it.

First of all, we must get out of the stands where we observe the process of writing from a distance — and after the fact — and get on the field where we can understand the pressures under which the writer operates. On the field, we will discover there is one principal negative force which keeps the writer from writing and four positive forces which help the writer move forward to a completed draft.

### Resistance to Writing

The negative force is *resistance* to writing, one of the great natural forces of nature. It may be called The Law of Delay: that writing which can be delayed, will be. Teachers and writers too often consider resistance to writing evil, when, in fact, it is necessary.

When I get an idea for a poem or an article or a talk or a short story, I feel myself consciously draw away from it. I seek procrastination and delay. There must be time for the seed of the idea to be nurtured in the mind. Far better writers than I have felt the same way. Over his writing desk Franz Kafka had one word, "Wait." William Wordsworth talked of the writer's "wise passiveness." Naturalist Annie Dillard recently said, "I'm waiting. I usually get my ideas in November, and I start writing in January. I'm waiting." Denise Levertov says, "If . . . somewhere in the vicinity there is a poem, then, no, I don't do anything about it, I wait."

Even the most productive writers are expert dawdlers, doers of unnecessary errands, seekers of interruptions — trials to their wives or husbands, friends, associates, and themselves. They sharpen well-pointed pencils and go out to buy more blank paper, rearrange offices, wander through libraries and bookstores, chop wood, walk, drive, make unnecessary calls, nap, daydream, and try not "consciously" to think about what they are going to write so they can think subconsciously about it.

Writers fear this delay, for they can name colleagues who have made a career of delay, whose great unwritten books will never be written, but, somehow, those writers who write must have the faith to sustain themselves through the necessity of delay.

### Forces for Writing

In addition to that faith, writers feel four pressures that move them forward towards the first draft.

The first is *increasing information* about the subject. Once a writer decides on a subject or accepts an assignment, information about the subject seems to attach itself to the writer. The writer's perception apparatus finds significance in what the writer observes or overhears or reads or thinks or remembers. The writer becomes a magnet for specific details, insights, anecdotes, statistics, connecting thoughts, references. The subject itself seems to take hold of the writer's experience, turning everything that happens to the writer into material. And this inventory of information creates pressure that moves the writer forward toward the first draft.

Usually the writer feels an *increasing concern* for the subject. The more a writer knows about the subject, the more the writer begins to feel about the subject. The writer cares that the subject be ordered and shared. The concern, which at first is a vague interest in the writer's mind, often becomes an obsession until it is communicated. Winston Churchill said, "Writing a book was an adventure. To begin with, it was a toy and amusement; then it became a mistress, and then a master. And then a tyrant."

The writer becomes aware of a *waiting audience*, potential readers who want or need to know what the writer has to say. Writing is an act of arrogance and communication. The writer rarely writes just for himself or herself, but for others who may be informed, entertained, or persuaded by what the writer has to say.

And perhaps most important of all, is the *approaching deadline*, which moves closer day by day at a terrifying and accelerating rate. Few writers publish without deadlines, which are imposed by others or by themselves. The deadline is real, absolute, stern, and commanding.

### Rehearsal for Writing

What the writer does under the pressure not to write and the four countervailing pressures to write is best described by the word *rehearsal*, which I first heard used by Dr. Donald Graves of the University of New Hampshire to describe what he saw young children doing as they began to write. He watched them draw what they would write and heard them, as we all have, speaking aloud what they might say on the page before they wrote. If you walk through editorial offices or a newspaper cityroom you will see lips moving and hear expert professionals muttering and whispering to themselves as they write. Rehearsal is a normal part of the writing process, but it took a trained observer such as Dr. Graves, to identify its significance.

Rehearsal covers much more than the muttering of struggling writers. As Dr. Graves points out, productive writers are "in a state of rehearsal all the time." Rehearsal usually begins with an unwritten dialogue within the writer's mind. "All of a sudden I discover what I have been thinking about a play," says Edward Albee. "This is usually between six months and a year before I actually sit down and begin typing it out." The writer thinks about characters or arguments, about plot or structure, about words and lines. The writer usually hears something which is similar to what Wallace Stevens must have heard as he walked through his insurance office working out poems in his head.

What the writer hears in his or her head usually evolves into note-taking. This may be simple brainstorming, the jotting down of random bits of information which may connect themselves into a pattern later on, or it may be journal-writing, a written dialogue between the writer and the subject. It may even become research recorded in a formal structure or note-taking.

Sometimes the writer not only talks to himself or herself, but to others — collaborators, editors, teachers, friends — working out the piece of writing in oral language with someone else who can enter into the process of discovery with the writer.

For most writers, the informal notes turn into lists, outlines, titles, leads, ordered fragments, all sketches of what later may be written, devices to catch a possible order that exists in the chaos of the subject.

In the final stage of rehearsal, the writer produces test drafts, written or unwritten. Sometimes they are called discovery drafts or trial runs or false starts that the writer doesn't think will be false. All writing is experimental, and the writer must come to the point where drafts are attempted in the writer's head and on paper.

Some writers seem to work more in their head, and others more on paper. Susan Sowers, a researcher at the University of New Hampshire, examining the writing processes of a group of graduate students found

a division . . . between those who make most discoveries during pre-writing and those who make most discoveries during writing and revision. The discoveries include the whole range from insights into personal issues to task-related organizational and content insight. The earlier the stage at which insights occur, the greater the drudgery associated with the writing-rewriting tasks. It may be that we resemble the young reflective and reactive writers. The less developmentally mature reactive writers enjoy writing more than reflective writers. They may use writing as a rehearsal for thinking just as young, reactive writers draw to rehearse writing. The younger and older reflective writers do not need to rehearse by drawing to write or by writing to think clearly or to discover new relationships and significant content.

This concept deserves more investigation. We need to know about both the reflective and reactive prewriting mode. We need to see if there are developmental changes in students, if they move from one mode to another as they mature, and we need to see if one mode is more important in certain writing tasks than others. We must, in every way possible, explore the significant writing stage of rehearsal which has rarely been described in the literature on the writing process.

## The Signals Which Say "Write"

During the rehearsal process, the experienced writer sees signals which tell the writer how to control the subject and produce a working first draft. The writer, Rebecca Rule, points out that in some cases when the subject is found, the way to deal with it is inherent in the subject. The subject itself is the signal. Most writers have experienced this quick passing through of the prewriting process. The line is given and the poem is clear; a character gets up and walks the writer through the story; the newspaperman attends a press conference, hears a quote, sees the lead and the entire structure of the article instantly. But many times the process is far less clear. The writer is assigned a subject or chooses one and then is lost.

E. B. White testifies, "I never knew in the morning how the day was going to develop. I was like a hunter hoping to catch sight of a rabbit." Denise Levertov says, "You can smell the poem before you see it." Most writers know these feelings but students who have never seen a rabbit dart across their writing desks or smelled a poem need to know the signals which tell them that a piece of writing is near.

What does the writer recognize which gives a sense of closure, a way of handling a diffuse and overwhelming subject? There seem to be eight principal signals to which writers respond.

One signal is *genre*. Most writers view the world as a fiction writer, a reporter, a poet, or an historian. The writer sees experience as a plot or a lyric poem or a news story or a chronicle. The writer uses such literary traditions to see and understand life.

"Ideas come to a writer because he has trained his mind to seek them out," says Brian Garfield. "Thus when he observes or reads or is exposed to a character or event, his mind sees the story possibilities in it and he begins to compose a dramatic structure in his mind. This process is incessant. Now and then it leads to something that will become a novel. But it's mainly an attitude: a way of looking at things; a habit of examining everything one perceives as potential material for a story."

Genre is a powerful but dangerous lens. It both clarifies and limits. The writer and the student must be careful not to see life merely in the stereotype form with which he or she is most familiar but to look at life with all of the possibilities of the genre in mind and to attempt to look at life through different genre.

Another signal the writer looks for is a *point of view*. This can be an opinion towards the subject or a position from which the writer — and the reader — studies the subject.

A tenement fire could inspire the writer to speak out against tenements, dangerous space-heating system, a fire-department budget cut. The fire might also be seen from the point of view of the people who were the victims or who escaped or who came home to find their home gone. It may be told from the point of view of a fireman, an arsonist, an insurance investigator, a fire-safety engineer, a real-estate planner, a housing inspector, a landlord, a spectator, as well as the victim. The list could go on.

Still another way the writer sees the subject is through *voice*. As the writer rehearses, in the writer's head and on paper, the writer listens to the sound of the language as a clue to the meaning of the subject and the writer's attitude toward that meaning. Voice is often the force which drives a piece of writing forward, which illuminates the subject for the writer and the reader.

A writer may, for example, start to write a test draft with detached unconcern and find that the language appearing on the page reveals anger or passionate concern. The writer who starts to write a solemn report of a meeting may hear a smile and then a laugh in his own words and go on to produce a humorous column.

*News* is an important signal for many writers who ask what the reader needs to know or would like to know. Those prolific authors of nature books, Lorus and Margery Milne, organize their books and each chapter in the books around what is new in the field. Between assignment and draft they are constantly looking for the latest news they can pass along to their readers. When they find what is new, then they know how to organize their writing.

Writers constantly wait for the *line* which is given. For most writers, there is an enormous difference between a thesis or an idea or a concept and an actual line, for the line itself has resonance. A single line can imply a voice, a tone, a pace, a whole way of treating a subject. Joseph Heller tells about the signal which produced his novel *Something Happened*.

> I begin with a first sentence that is independent of any conscious preparation. Most often nothing comes out of it: a sentence will come to mind that doesn't lead to a second sentence. Sometimes it will lead to thirty sentences which then come to a dead end. I was alone on the deck. As I sat there worrying and wondering what to do, one of those first lines suddenly came to mind: "In the office in which I work, there are four people of whom I am afraid. Each of these four people is afraid of five people." Immediately, the lines presented a whole explosion of possibilities and choices — characters (working in a corporation), a tone, a mood of anxiety, or of insecurity. In that first hour (before someone came along and asked me to go to the beach) I knew the beginning, the ending, most of the middle, the whole scene of that particular "something" that was going to happen; I knew about the brain-damaged child, and especially, of course, about Bob Slocum, my protagonist, and what frightened him, that he wanted to be liked, that his immediate hope was to be allowed to make a three-minute speech at the company convention. Many of the actual lines throughout the book came to me — the entire "something happened" scene with those solar plexus lines (beginning with the doctor's statement and ending with "Don't tell my wife" and the rest of them) all coming to me in the first hour on that Fire Island deck. Eventually I found a different opening chapter with a different first line ("I get the willies when I see closed doors") but I kept the original which had spurred everything to start off the second section.

Newspapermen are able to write quickly and effectively under pressure because they become skillful at identifying a lead, that first line — or two or three — which will inform and entice the reader and which, of course, also gives the writer control over the subject. As an editorial writer, I found that finding the title first gave me control over the subject. Each title became, in effect, a pre-draft, so that in listing potential titles I would come to one which would be a signal as to how the whole editorial could be written.

Poets and fiction writers often receive their signals in terms of an *image*. Sometimes this image is static; other times it is a moving picture in the writer's mind. When Gabriel Garcia Marquez was asked what the starting point of his novels was, he answered, "A completely visual image . . . the starting point of *Leaf Storm* is an old man taking his grandson to a funeral, in *No One Writes to the Colonel*, it's an old man waiting, and in *One Hundred Years*, an old man taking his grandson to the fair to find out what ice is." William Faulkner was quoted as saying, "It begins with a character, usually, and once he stands up on his feet and begins to move, all I do is trot along behind him with a paper and pencil trying to keep up long enough to put down what he says and does." It's a comment which seems facetious — if you're not a fiction writer. Joyce Carol Oates adds, "I visualize the characters completely; I have heard their dialogue, I know how they speak, what they want, who they are, nearly everything about them."

Although image has been testified to mostly by imaginative writers, where it is obviously most appropriate, I think research would show that nonfiction writers often see an image as the signal. The person, for example, writing a memo about a manufacturing procedure may see the assembly line in his or her mind. The polition arguing for a pension law may see a person robbed of a pension, and by seeing that person know how to organize a speech or the draft or a new law.

Many writers know they are ready to write when they see a *pattern* in a subject. This pattern is usually quite different from what we think of as an outline, which is linear and goes from beginning to end. Usually the writer sees something which might be called a gestalt, which is, in the world of the dictionary, "a unified physical, psychological, or symbolic configuration having properties that cannot be derived from its parts." The writer usually in a moment sees the entire piece of writing as a shape, a form, something that is more than all of its parts, something that is entire and is represented in his or her mind, and probably on paper, by a shape.

Marge Piercy says, "I think that the beginning of fiction, of the story, has to do with the perception of pattern in event." Leonard Gardner, in talking of his fine novel *Fat City*, said, "I had a definite design in mind. I had a sense of circle . . . of closing the circle at the end." John Updike says, "I really begin with some kind of solid, coherent image, some notion of the shape of the book and even of its texture. *The Poorhouse Fair* was meant to have a sort of wide shape. *Rabbit, Run* was kind of zigzag. *The Centaur* was sort of a sandwich."

We have interviews with imaginative writers about the writing process, but rarely interviews with science writers, business writers, political writers, journalists, ghost writers, legal writers, medical writers — examples of effective writers who use language to inform and persuade. I am convinced that such research would reveal that they also see patterns or gestalts which carry them from idea to draft..

"It's not the answer that enlightens but the question," says Ionesco. This insight into what the writer is looking for is one of the most significant considerations in trying to understand the free-writing process. A most significant book based on more than ten years of study of art students, *The Creative Vision, A Longitudinal Study of Problem-Finding in Art*, by Jacob W. Getzels and Mihaly Csikszentmihalyi, has documented how the most creative students are those who come up with the *problem* to be solved rather than a quick answer. The signal to the creative person may well be the problem, which will be solved through the writing.

We need to take all the concepts of invention from classical rhetoric and combine them with what we know from modern psychology, from studies of creativity, from writers' testimony about the prewriting process. Most of all, we need to observe successful students and writers during the prewriting process, and to debrief them to find out what they do when they move effectively from assignment or idea to completed first draft. Most of all, we need to move from failure-centered research to research which defines what happens when the writing goes well, just what is the process followed by effective student and professional writers. We know far too little about the writing process.

## Implications for Teaching Writing

Our speculations make it clear that there are significant implications for the teaching of writing in a close examination of what happens between receiving an assignment or finding a subject and beginning a completed first draft. We may need, for example, to reconsider our attitude toward those who delay writing. We may, in fact, need to force many of our glib, hair-trigger student writers to slow down, to daydream, to waste time, but not to avoid a reasonable deadline.

We certainly should allow time within the curriculum for prewriting, and we should work with our students to help them understand the process of rehearsal, to allow them the experience of rehearsing what they will write in their minds, on the paper, and with collaborators.

We should also make our students familiar with the signals they may see during the rehearsal process which will tell them that they are ready to write, that they have a way of dealing with their subject.

The prewriting process is largely invisible; it takes place within the writer's head or on scraps of paper that are rarely published. But we must understand that such a process takes place, that it is significant, and that it can be made clear to our students. Students who are not writing, or not writing well, may have a second chance if they are able to experience the writers' counsel to write before writing.

# How to Completely Individualize a Writing Program

by WILLIAM A. CLARK
*Shrewsbury, Mass., Public Schools*

> Talking to students about writing doesn't make them better writers.
> Students learn to write by writing.
> Therefore: Students should write more.
>
> The more students write, the more papers teachers have to correct.
> It is hard to motivate students to write anyway.
> Therefore: Students don't write very much.

THESE SYLLOGISMS CATCH the great dilemma of teaching writing in a nutshell. The predicament cries out for an approach that is simple, is relatively convenient, and works. Maybe anyone who splits an infinitive, right in the title, has no business suggesting an approach. Especially if he seems to consistently do it. Double-especially if he is an *ex*-English teacher now defected to the ranks of administration. But I have used the approach that follows several times, with groups of high ability, low ability, mixed abilities, and seemingly no ability. With all of them it works, if you will accept my rigorously unscientific measures of effectiveness:

*Students write more, much more, than they ever did before during an equivalent span of time.*

*They do it with little hassle, at least compared to groups I have taught in more traditional ways.*

*The writing is more interesting to read.*

With this approach I found myself consistently looking forward to reading papers, a luxury that I, for one, have enjoyed all too seldom during my teaching career. Perhaps many teachers would not consider this as evidence of success. I once heard a distinguished writing professor say only half-facetiously that when a student submits a dull paper, the teacher should ask the student to come in and read the paper back aloud while the teacher yawns. An extreme move, I admit. But the fact is that students know when they're writing interesting stuff — they're interested in it and excited about it themselves.

Best of all, students are enthusiastic. Perhaps the only scientific way of judging students' enthusiasm is to wrap blood-pressure straps around their arms and monitor the dials. But teachers are a supersensitive lot, and every one I've met (me included) has hairy little antennae that pick up classroom vibrations with split-second speed. I *know* when something is working in my classroom.

To begin a writing program, you take each student where he is. Most teachers will subscribe to this starting point, without being very clear about what it means. I'm afraid that to many teachers it means placing each student's writing on a continuum from *Perfectly Awful* to *Supergood*. Then the goal is to move the student along the continuum. One catch among many is that judgments of *Good* and *Bad*, and of student placement in between, are based on the *teacher's* perceptions. And we've all done those little experiments in which a group of teachers read the same composition and come up with wildly different assessments of it.

A writing program has to start with the *student's* perception of where he is. Therefore, the early stages have to emphasize the importance of the individual student's uniqueness and the teacher's willingness — even determination — to accept it. On the first day, I "lecture." I take students for a ten-minute walk outside the school building. I point out things that interest me and move me to verbalization: cars in the student parking lot, the uniform rows of school windows looking out from uniform rows of classrooms, the students inside staring at us outside, the absence of student activity outside the building, the flag on the pole, etc. I suggest how these things trigger off associations that are significant to me and that I would like to write about. Each student of course sees things I don't see and makes connections that no other person would make, and I encourage anyone who feels like it to do so as we walk. The point of the tour is that any 10-minute observation period in anyone's day will provide raw materials for completely personalized associations.

Back inside, they do the first (and last) canned writing assignment: Write a quick (5 minute) description of the view outside the classroom window. A description of anything else would do as well, as long as everyone describes the same thing. Then I read each one aloud, divulging no author's name, commenting about how each individual perceived the scene in a unique way. This one sees geometric patterns, another catalogues the phenomena methodically from left to right, still another puts the description in a framework of it's-beautiful-out-there-and-we're-stuck-in-here. Every description comes naturally out of the author's way of looking at this piece of his world. No mention is made of the quality of the writing. Every way of perceiving is valid, and no one perception is more valid than another.

Whether or not a teacher uses this particular strategy of reading back descriptions, I cannot overemphasize the importance of the process of validating each student's uniqueness. Importance, that is, to the teacher, because it commits the teacher to a public stance. (How the students take it depends on your subsequent actions: They are conditioned to play it cool and see if the teacher lives up to his promise.) Faced with a batch of papers, many teachers have a tendency to classify (Good and Bad; A, B, or C; those that need a lot of revision, those that don't, etc.) — that is, to match them against some standard. But the validation process asks the teacher to avoid mental subsets of any kind and to consider each student's vision as unique. Incidentally, it's surprisingly easy to read back papers and articulate the unique point of view without any preparation. After a while you can read back the papers of five classes, thirty students each, and report 150 different ways of seeing the same scene. If a student tries to record the unique way he perceives things, he is writing "individually." He is into an individualized writing program.

So far all this has been preparatory. The day-to-day work of the course depends on whether this is a course in writing only or a "Kitchen Sink" English course. I've done it both ways, and while I prefer the writing-only course, this approach can be woven in and around literature, spelling, grammar, speech, and all the other pieces that once led me to put up a horrendous bulletin board display entitled "English Is a Many-Splendored Thing." In the writing-only course, students write a pre-determined number of rough drafts, say ten in a half-year course. They use any writing modes they wish, any subjects they wish. This freedom is hard for students to handle at first. "I can't think of anything to write about." (Translation: What do you really want me to write about?) I make suggestions, and plenty of them. I even give specific "assignments," complete with examples, instructions, advice — always ending with, "But you don't have to write that if you don't want to."

It is important, I think, to persist in not telling students what to write about or what mode to use. Once you succumb to the pressure, the student flips back to the same old please-the-teacher channel and both of you are licked. Persist and you will find that one by one most students will accept their freedom and finally exult in it. Since there is almost no group instruction, the teacher is free to walk around and confer. But these early "what-do-I-write-about conferences" must reinforce the idea that the student is to write out of his perceptions, not yours. The teacher has to find out what the student has been doing and thinking about lately, maybe to have him recall, if necessary, one of his recent 10-minute walks. Using this as raw material, the teacher helps the student discover his own topic. And he has to write about *his* topic; the zappiest topic you pick out of the air to hand him will be your topic, not his. Some students find it helpful to write a detailed account of that ten minutes from their day. Out of that the teacher can help the student find other subjects and suggest alternate ways of handling those subjects (poetry, sketch, interior monologue, etc.).

The early goal, then, is to churn out rough drafts. Emphasis is clearly not on quality but on finding one's own voice, finding out what one wants to say. Drafts are incomplete, tentative, just barely legible enough for someone else to read. They are not graded. Periodically (usually at the end of a marking period) we invoke the delightful strategy offered by Don Murray. The student selects a few of his papers that *he* thinks are most promising and polishes them for a grade. Between the drafts and the hand-ins comes the nitty-gritty of revision.

Students are encouraged to get off a number of rough drafts before revising any of them. Since they know that in the end only a few of their papers will be graded, and then only after plenty of revision, a beautiful thing happens: They begin to feel free to experiment with their rough drafts. If they want to try a crazy stream-of-consciousness technique or imitate Salinger or write a parody, they are free to try it. If an experiment doesn't work out, there is no penalty — they just won't select it later for handing in.

It is frequently hard for a teacher to accept (in any sense of the word) some of the experimental efforts, especially when an effort somehow doesn't come off. In some papers it's hard to know what the student was trying to do, especially when he didn't really *do* what he was trying to do. After I read a student's rough draft I invariably ask him the same question: What do you think is the best thing about this paper? The question is intentionally ambiguous. It might be interpreted to mean, "What do you like best about it?" or "Which section do you think is best?" or "Which idea in it do you really like and were you trying to get at?"

A few years ago I was in a small group of experienced writing teachers at an NDEA Institute. We had all written a quick, short paper on anything we liked, with no time for revision. Sitting aroung a table, we all read dittoed copies of everyone's drafts. The leader asked us to suggest ways each paper could be improved. I had already figured the way I wanted to improve mine. What surprised me was that not one of those experienced and competent teachers suggested what I was thinking of. Their suggestions were good, but those teachers weren't *me*, and they couldn't possibly have figured out what would be the most appropriate direction for me.

So I ask the students, "What do *you* think is the best thing about your draft?" And whatever they say (incredibly, they almost always *do* say), whether I see any possibilities in their selection or NOT, I accept it and try to help them build on it. One boy wrote a paean to his girl friend, with two pages of delicious and loving physical description of her, and a final innocuous sentence or two about how he felt when he was with her. Yet he told me he felt the ending was the best part. I was surprised, even disappointed, but apparently the description part wasn't what he wanted to write. Perhaps he thought papers about people *should* start with a physical description — I don't know. Anyhow, we talked for a while about how he felt when he was near her, and he seemed relieved and happy to go back and redo the paper the way *he* wanted it. As it turned out, he did include portions of the physical description in his final draft, but in a context that was his own creation.

One of the ironies of teaching writing is that most teachers give of their expertise when the student needs it least. They give a lot of help before the student starts to write, and after the student has written, but too little during the process. Once the student has done a rough draft and has freely committed himself to doing a revision, he then truly needs (and wants) a teacher's help. At least most students do. When you individualize there are precious few generalizations you can make that apply to all students in a class. Some want help infrequently, and then only with pressing problems. Some want help with wording, some with grammar or spelling, some with organization. Some want no help at all. So I spend most of the class time sitting with students providing on-the-spot help. There are even some who want a draft completely red-penciled in the good old-fashioned way. I invite them to submit a second draft, still in pencil, for this service.

Of course you can sneak in some unsolicited advice at times, if it somehow is in the context of something the student has solicited. An interesting phenomenon is that a student's requests will change as time goes on. If the door is left open, he will tend to ask for the type of help he feels himself ready for. A typical pattern for many — though not all — is to ask for increasingly more help with mechanics, as concerns grow for "getting it just right."

A problem that arises in every class I have taught is the boy who wants to write only about cars. But why discourage him? That's clearly where he's at, at this stage of his life, for perfectly understandable psychological and sociological reasons. (I remember during my first year of teaching all I thought about or read about or wrote about was school.) The teacher can suggest different ways of writing about cars. The student can, for instance, write for audiences with varying knowledge of cars, from his car-ignorant teacher to his car-sophisticated friends. He may enjoy writing a glossary of technical car terms, to flaunt his special knowledge and get some control over a world so fascinating to him. But if his world is mainly populated with cars, then he ought to write about them.

Many experts on the teaching of writing place great emphasis on having students "correct" each other's papers. Moffett suggests dividing a class into small groups in which students read their papers and provide mutual feedback. An excellent idea, though I must confess I've never had much success at making it work. The groups seem to be either unduly tough on each other, or unduly accepting of everything they read. I prefer the constant informal swapping of papers that inevitably goes on when the teacher walks around the room talking with individuals and the atmosphere is not one of control from the front. Students, especially those who are beginning to build confidence in their own perceptions, hunger for supportive advice, and they know which classmates will provide it and which ones probably won't. Of course there should be periodic "publishing" of student writing. My favorite way is the dittoed class "literary magazine," which includes at least one selection by each student and is distributed just within the class (with extra copies for the students to hand out to anybody else). A copy to each administrator in the school is a dandy move.

I don't mean to suggest that the teacher should spend all his class time walking around talking to students. Sometimes he has to read papers. And he should himself do some writing, for a lot of reasons that I guess are obvious. One that may not be so obvious is that he really gets to know what students are going through. Teachers do scandalously little writing, except for term papers, and it won't be term papers these students are writing. (Though a perfectly legitimate activity in this class is for a student to write a term paper for another class.) Ask a student or two to read your drafts and react. It feels good later on when inevitably you find a student is having a problem you had, and you can say how you solved it.

As the end of the marking period approaches, all energies are focused on revising a few drafts for official "handing in." The revision of some papers may have started way back near the beginning of the term and have gone through several stages. Before a paper is ready, the student can exhaust the possibilities for advice and suggestions from teacher and classmates and can be reasonably sure that his final draft represents the best work he is capable of. There will be no surprises when he gets it back. When he finally does hand it in, all the learning about writing he is to do during the program will be completed, so that by the act of submitting the paper for a grade he is merely paying his respects to a grading system he is stuck with. This is the only time of real work for the teacher, because there is suddenly a big pile of papers to read all at once. But there is little commenting to be done, and the grades should be delightfully high.

I haven't said much about quality in the students' writing. The quality of their papers does improve, markedly so, but not in ways I could have predicted or planned for with any accuracy. Behavioral objectives would be absurd for such a program. Certainly this approach won't insure that a student gets a balance of experience in writing essays, short stories, book reports, and all the other types of writing, or that a student will learn all the elements of composition in the rhetoric handbook. One eleventh grade girl spent a whole term working on one long, long short story. It wasn't a very good story even by the standard of the class, though it was a much better story at the end of the term than at the beginning. But she found her voice. She felt a new confidence in her ability to use that voice as she went on to other courses which demanded other kinds of writing.

Writing, it seems to me, cannot be "learned" in the same sense as one can learn square roots or punctuation or typewriting. One never really completes the process of learning to write. The technical skill is intimately tied up with one's self-confidence, self-image, and self-growth. Somewhere in the school experience, every student needs to have the chance to experience that kind of growth.

# Time for Questions: Getting Started

*WHAT CAN I DO for students who say they don't have anything to write about?*

Students can mean many things when they say this. They may mean that they don't have "appropriate" topics; they can mean that they're afraid that if they invest energy in writing, they will be criticized; they could mean that they don't have *enough* to write about on any topic.

One way to help students discover topics and information about topics is to have them make lists. Here's a sequence you can go through:

1. Ask students to write an "authority list" — 25 (or any other number you choose) possible topics: experiences, hobbies, opinions, things that annoy them, people they admire, places they've visited, books they've read, movies they've seen, sports they play, and so on.

2. Once the list is completed put a star beside the topic the student likes best.

3. Students should pair up and ask each other questions about the topic each has chosen.

4. After the interviews, each student should make a list of key words — details, names, quotes, examples, physical descriptions that they might use to write about the topic.

5. Write about the topic.

This procedure slows down the composing process for students. Too often students have little to write about because they do not take time to inventory their own knowlege — they don't yet know what they know.

This procedure also gets the student talking about his or her topic, and talking helps students know what they know. But if students are to talk teachers must be willing to listen, and there are volumes of research studies to show that we don't do it well. I find that I get the best results when I begin with a general invitation to talk — "Could you tell me more about X?" The student will often begin with a rambling kind of list; then something will click, there will be animation in the voice; and the student senses that an oral text is being created, one that can be transformed into a written text.

My most vivid memory of this process involved a student of mine who had worked diligently for half a semester and had produced nothing that anyone would want to read. This particular week she had written on her hometown in Vermont, and the paper was like the ones she had written before, mechanical and lifeless. I asked her to tell me something about her hometown, and she talked for a while, but nothing clicked, nothing was added that could enliven her paper. Near the end of the conference, she picked up a postcard and said, "Look what I bought in the bookstore." It was Norman Rockwell's picture of Rosie the Rivetter painted during World War II. "That's my mother."

It literally was her mother, who had posed for Rockwell. Not only had her mother posed, but many others in her town had also posed. And in typical New England fashion many of these people still lived in the hometown so dully described in her paper. So her next paper involved interviews with these people, their memories of Rockwell. A splendid paper she had talked her way into.

*I have students who can find topics but their writing is painfully slow. What can I do about it?*

Many students labor over their writing because they try to get it *right* the first time. I had a student describe her process as follows:

> I decided to write about my grandfather. "Grandfather was a woodsman." I began. Was he? Actually he was also an applepicker and a carpenter. I added those to the line. Now it was too long. I should concentrate on one subject I said to myself. Was it "woodsman" or "woodsmen?" I looked it up in the dictionary. "Woodsman" was correct. I reread the first sentence; it sounded OK. Now for number 2.

It's painful to imagine someone continuing this way. William Stafford, the poet, offers some good advice for students who put themselves under this kind of pressure: "If I am to keep writing, I cannot bother to insist on high standards. I must get into action and not let anything stop me, or even slow me much."

One way for students to "get into action" is to ask them to free-write regularly. Initially I ask my students to write for 10 minutes on any topic, and when the time is up I ask them simply to count the number of words they have written. Many are surprised that they can write the equivalent of a typed page in 10 minutes. As the term progresses I regularly ask them to write at the beginning of class — sometimes on a topic I assign, sometimes on a topic they choose.

Many students lack fluency because they have not had to compose regularly. Bryant Fillion in a later article in this collection reports that the amount of writing students do can vary wildly from year to year. And Mina Shaughnessy estimates that many basic writers do almost no writing. They are caught in a powerful dilemma: because they have difficulty writing they are not asked to do much, and because they are not asked to do much writing, it becomes increasingly more difficult. As students write more frequently, they not only develop more ease in writing, they also begin to write when they are not writing. They think about what they might write when they ride the bus or walk the dog. They begin to resemble James Thurber who would sometimes mumble incomprehensibly at the dinner table. If guests were present, Thurber's wife would turn to them and explain, "You'll have to excuse him. He's writing."

*What kind of prewriting activities would help students with expository or informational writing?*

It's often useful to try a variation on the listing activity above. But this time students might be asked to write lists of questions about the topic, not just a few, but a large number. The first questions on the list will be the obvious ones; the later ones are likely to be more interesting. As students plan they might consider the order in which readers would like questions answered.

Many students have also found mapping to be useful in showing the relationships among ideas. To construct a map the writer circles the key word of the piece. If I were writing a chapter on helping students to begin writing, I might begin with "getting started" circled:

Then I would create some branches:

Then there are areas or points that connect with each of these branches:

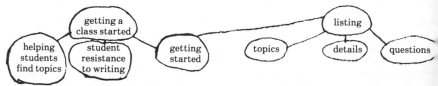

And so on. Not every branch will be used in the writing, but the method helps lay out possibilities and connections in a way that an outline does not. For a more extensive description of this method see Donald Murray's *Write to Learn* (Holt, Rinehart, and Winston).

*How can I get students to write term papers that don't bore me to tears?*

Most "term papers" are too long; the student has to stretch to make the assigned length, and, as a consequence uses almost all of the information gathered. There is no selection process — no throwing away. Six to eight typewritten, double-spaced pages is a maximum length.

But the biggest problem with research papers is the inability of students to transform researched information into their own language. After all, their sources say it so much better than they can. There are two things you can do to deal with this problem. At points in the writing ask students to write "What I Have Learned" papers, quick free-writings without benefit of notes, where the student says in his or her own words what has been learned from the research. In this way, the student is freed from the language of the sources.

Students can also be encouraged to select topics where they can interview an expert. A student interested in emergency medicine could interview an ambulance attendant; someone interested in farm foreclosures could interview farmers or loan officers of banks. Good advice on interviewing can be found in William Zinnser's *On Writing Well*. I would also suggest Kenneth Macrorie's *Searching Writing* which has excellent ideas for an I-Search paper where a student moves into the community to gather information.

# Suggestions for Further Reading:
## Getting Started

Elbow, Peter. *Writing without Teachers* (New York: Oxford University Press, 1973).

Flower, Linda and John Hayes. "The Cognition of Discovery: Defining a Rhetorical Problem," *College Composition and Communication*, 31 (February, 1980): 21-32.

Flower, Linda. *Problem-solving Strategies for Writing* second edition (New York: Harcourt Brace, 1984).

Irmscher, William. *Teaching Expository Writing* (New York: Holt, Rinehart, and Winston, 1979).

Kirby, Dan and Tom Liner. *Inside Out: Strategies for Teaching Writing as a Developmental Process* (Montclair, N.J.: Boynton/Cook, 1980).

Macrorie, Kenneth. *Searching Writing* (Montclair, N.J.: Boynton/Cook, 1980).

Macrorie, Kenneth. *Telling Writing* third edition (Montclair, N.J.: Boynton/Cook, 1980).

Moffett, James. *Active Voice: A Writing Program Across the Curriculum* (Montclair, N.J.: Boynton/Cook, 1981).

Murray, Donald. "Writing as Process: How Writing Finds Its Own Meaning" in his *Learning by Teaching* (Montclair, N.J.: Boynton/Cook, 1982).

Rose, Mike. "Rigid Rules, Inflexible Plans, and the Stifling of Language: A Cognitivist Analysis of Writer's Block," *College Composition and Communication*, 31 (December, 1980): 389-401.

Stafford, William. *Writing the Australian Crawl* (Ann Arbor, Mich.: University of Michigan Press, 1978).

Welty, Eudora. *One Writer's Beginning* (Cambridge, Mass.: Harvard University Press, 1983).

Zinnser, William. *On Writing Well* second edition (New York: Harper and Row, 1980).

# Responding

# Teaching the Other Self
## *The Writer's First Reader*

by DONALD MURRAY
*University of New Hampshire*

W E URGE OUR students to write for others, but writers report they write for themselves. "I write for me," says Edward Albee. "The audience of me." Teachers of composition make a serious mistake if they consider such statements a matter of artistic ego alone.

The testimony of writers that they write for themselves opens a window on an important part of the writing process. If we look through that window we increase our understanding of the process and become more effective teachers of writing.

"I am my own first reader," says Issac Bashevis Singer. "Writers write for themselves and not for their readers," declares Rebecca West, "and that art has nothing to do with communication between person and person, only with communication between different parts of a person's mind." "I think the audience an artist imagines," states Vladimir Nabokov, "when he imagines that sort of thing, is a room filled with people wearing his own mask." Edmund Blunden adds, "I don't think I have ever written for anybody except the other in one's self."

The act of writing might be described as a conversation between two workmen muttering to each other at the workbench. The self speaks, the other self listens and responds. The self proposes, the other self considers. The self makes, the other self evaluates. The two selves collaborate: a problem is spotted, discussed, defined; solutions are proposed, rejected, suggested, attempted, tested, discarded, accepted.

This process is described in that fine German novel, *The German Lesson*, by Siegfried Lenz, when the narrator in the novel watches the painter Nansen, at work. "And, as always when he was at work he was talking. He didn't talk to himself, he talked to someone by the name of Balthasar, who stood beside him, his Balthasar, who only he could see and hear, with whom he chatted and argued and

65

whom he sometimes jabbed with his elbow, so hard that even we, who couldn't see any Balthasar, would suddenly hear the invisible bystander groan, or, if not groan, at least swear. The longer we stood there behind him, the more we began to believe in the existence of that Balthasar who made himself perceptible by a sharp intake of breath or a hiss of disappointment. And still the painter went on confiding in him, only to regret it a moment later."

Study this activity at the workbench within the skull and you might say that the self writes, the other self reads. But it is not reading as we usually consider it, the decoding of a completed text. It is a sophisticated reading that monitors writing before it is made, as it is made, and after it is made.

The term monitor is significant, for the reading during writing involves awareness on many levels and includes the opportunity for change. And when that change is made then everything must be read again to see how the change affects the reading.

The writer, as the text evolves, reads fragments of language as well as completed units of language, what isn't on the page as well as what is on the page, what should be left out as well as what should be put in. Even patterns and designs — sketches of possible relationships between pieces of information or fragments of rhetoric or language — that we do not usually consider language are read and discussed by the self and the other self.

It is time researchers in the discipline called English bridge the gulf between the reading researcher and the writing researcher. There are now many trained writing researchers who can collaborate with the trained researcher in reading, for the act of writing is inseparable from the act of reading. You can read without writing, but you can't write without reading. The reading skills required, however, to decode someone else's finished text may be quite different from the reading skills required to chase a wisp of thinking until it grows into a completed thought.

To follow thinking that has not yet become thought, the writer's other self has to be an explorer, a map maker. The other self scans the entire territory, forgetting, for the moment, questions of order or language. The writer/explorer looks for the draft's horizons. Once the writer has scanned the larger vision of the territory, it may be possible to trace a trail that will get the writer from here to there, from meaning identified to meaning clarified. Questions of order are now addressed, but questions of language still delayed. Finally, the writer/explorer studies the map in detail to spot the hazards that lie along the trail, the hidden swamps of syntax, the underbrush of verbiage, the voice found, lost, found again.

Map making and map reading are among man's most complex cognitive tasks. Eventually the other self learns to monitor the always changing relationship between where the writer is and where the writer intended to go. The writer/explorer stops, looks ahead, considers and reconsiders the trail and the ways to get around the obstacles that block that trail.

There is only one way the student can learn map reading — and that is in the field. Books and lecturers may help, but only after the student writer has been out in the bush will the student understand the kind of reading essential for the exploration of thinking. The teacher has to be a guide who doesn't lead so much as stand behind the young explorer, pointing out alternatives only at the moment of panic. Once the writer/explorer has read one map and made the trip from meaning intended to meaning realized, will the young writer begin to trust the other self and have faith it will know how to read other trails through other territories.

The reading writer — map maker and map reader — reads the word, the line, the sentence, the paragraph, the page, the entire text. This constant back-and-forth reading monitors the multiple complex relationships between all the elements in writing. Recursive scanning — or reviewing and previewing — is beginning to be documented during revision by Sondra Perl, Nancy Sommers, and others. But further and more sophisticated investigation will, I believe, show that the experienced writer is able, through the writer's other self, to read what has gone before and what may come afterward during the writing that is done before there is a written text, and during the writing that produces an embryonic text.

I think we can predict some of the functions that are performed by the other self during the writing process.

- The other self tracks the activity that is taking place. Writing, in a sense, does not exist until it is read. The other self records the evolving text.

- The other self gives the self the distance that is essential for craft. This distance, the craftperson's step backwards, is a key element in that writing that is therapeutic for the writer.

- The other self provides an evolving context for the writer. As the writer adds, cuts, or records, the other self keeps track of how each change affects the draft.

- The other self articulates the process of writing, providing the writer with an engineering history of the developing text, a technical resource that records the problems faced and the solutions that were tried and rejected, not yet tried, and the one that is in place.

- The other self is the critic who is continually looking at the writing to see if, in the writer's phrase, "it works."

- The other self also is the supportive colleague to the writer, the chap who commiserates and encourages, listens sympathetically to the writer's complaints and reminds the writer of past success. The deeper we get into the writing process the more we may discover how affective concerns govern the cognitive, for writing is an intellectual activity carried on in an emotional environment, a precisely engineered sailboat trying to hold course in a vast and stormy Atlantic. The captain has to deal with fears as well as compass readings.

We shall have to wait for perceptive and innovative research by teams of reading and writing researchers to document the complex kind of reading that is done during the writing process. But fortunately, we do not have to wait for the results of such research to make use of the other self in the teaching of writing.

The other self can be made articulate. It has read the copy as it was being created and knows the decisions that were made to produce the draft. This does not mean that they were all conscious decisions in the sense that the writer articulated what was being done, but even instinctive or subconscious editorial decisions can be articulated retrospectively.

Many teachers of writing, especially those who are also teachers of literature, are deeply suspicious of the testimony of writers about their own writing. It may be that the critic feels that he or she knows more than the writer, that the testimony of writers is too simple to be of value. But I have found in my own work that what students and professional writers say about their own writing process is helpful and makes sense in relation to the text.

Writing is, after all, a rational act; the writing self was monitored by the reading self during the writing process. The affective may well control or stimulate or limit the cognitive, but writing is thinking, and a thinking act can, most of the time, be recreated in rational terms. The tennis pro may return a serve instinctively, but instinct is, in part, internalized consciousness, and if you ask the pro about that particular return the experienced player will be able to describe what was done and why. If the player thought consciously at the time of the serve, the ball would sail by. The return was a practiced, learned act made spontaneous by experience, and it can be described and explained after the fact.

This retroactive understanding of what was done makes it possible for the teacher not only to teach the other self but recruit the other self to assist in the teaching of writing. The teacher brings the other self into existence, and then works with that other self so that, after the student has graduated, the other self can take over the function of teacher.

When the student speaks and the student and teacher listen they are both informed about the nature of the writing process that produced the draft. This is the point at which the teacher knows what needs to be taught or reinforced one step at a time, and the point at which the student knows what needs to be done in the next draft.

Listening is not a normal composition teacher's skill. We tell and they listen. But to make effective use of the other self the teacher and the student must listen together.

This is done most efficiently in conference. But before the conference at the beginning of the course the teacher must explain to the class exactly why the student is to speak first. I tell my students that I'm going to do as little as possible to interfere with their learning. It is their job to read the text, to evaluate it, to decide how it can be improved so that they will be able to write when I am not there. I point out that the ways in which they write are different, their problems and solutions are different, and that I am a resource to help them find their own way. I will always attempt to underteach so that they can overlearn.

I may read the paper before the conference or during the conference, but the student will always speak first in the conference. I have developed a repertoire of questions — what surprised you? what's working best? what are you going to do next? — but I rarely use them. The writing conference is not a special occasion. The student comes to get my response to the work, and I give my response to the student's response. I am teaching the other self.

The more inexperienced the student and the less comprehensible the text, the more helpful the writer's comments. Again and again with remedial students I am handed a text that I simply can not understand. I do not know what it is supposed to say. I can not discover a pattern of organization. I can not understand the language. But when the writer tells me what the writer was doing, when the other self is allowed to speak, I find that the text was produced rationally. The writer followed misunderstood instruction, inappropriate principles, or logical processes that did not work.

Most students, for example, feel that if you want to write for a large audience you should write in general terms, in large abstractions. They must be told that is logical; but it simply doesn't work. The larger the audience, the more universal we want our message to be, the more specific we must become. It was E.B. White who reminded us, "Don't write about Man, write about *a* man."

When the teacher listens to the student, the conference can be short. The student speaks about the process that produced the draft or about the draft itself. The teacher listens, knowing that the effective teacher must teach where the student is, not where the teacher wishes the student was, then scans or rescans the draft to confirm, adjust, or disagree with the student's comments.

One thing the responsive teacher, the teacher who listens to the student first then to the text, soon learns is that the affective usually controls the cognitive, and affective responses have to be dealt with first. I grew used to this with students, but during the past two years I have also worked with professionals on some of the best newspapers in the country, and I have found that it is even more true of published writers. Writers' feelings control the environment in which the mind functions. Unless the teacher knows this environment the teaching will be off target.

In conference, for example, the majority of men have been socialized to express a false confidence in their writing. The teacher who feels these men are truly confident will badly misread the writer's other self. The behavior of women in conference is changing, but not fast enough. Most women still express the false modesty about their accomplishments that society has said is appropriate for women. Again the teacher must recognize and support the other self that knows how good the work really is.

I am constantly astonished when I see drafts of equal accomplishment, but with writer evaluations that are miles apart. One student may say, "This is terrible. I can't write. I think I'd better drop the course." And right after that on a similar paper a student says, "I never had so much fun writing before. I think this is really a good paper. Do you think I should become a writer?"

Many students, of course, have to deal first with these feelings about the draft — or about writing itself. The conference teacher should listen to these comments, for they often provide important clues to why the student is writing — or avoiding writing — in a particular way.

The instructor who wishes to teach the other self must discuss the text with that other self in less despairing or elated tones. Too often the inexperienced conference teacher goes to the polar extreme and offers the despairing student absolute praise and the confident student harsh criticism. In practice, the effective conference teacher does not deal in praise or criticism. All texts can be improved, and the instructor discusses with the student what is working and can be made to work better, and what isn't working and how it might be made to work.

As the student gets by the student's feelings, the concerns become more cognitive. At first the students, and the ineffective writing teacher, focus on the superficial, the most obvious problems of language or manuscript preparation. But the teacher, through questioning, can reorient the student to the natural hierarchy of editorial concerns.

These questions over a series of conferences may evolve from "What's the single most important thing you have to say?" to "What questions is the reader going to ask you and when are they going to be asked?" to "Where do you hear the voice come through strongest?"

The students will discover, as the teacher models an ideal other self, that the largest questions of content, meaning, or focus have to be dealt with first. Until there is a clear meaning the writer can not order the information that supports that meaning or leads towards it. And until the meaning and its supporting structure is clear the writer can not make the decisions about voice and language that clarify and communicate that meaning. The other self has to monitor many activities and make sure that the writing self reads what is being monitored in an effective sequence.

Sometimes teachers who are introduced to teaching the other self feel that listening to this student first means they can not intervene. That is not true. This is not a do-your-own-thing kind of teaching. It is a demanding teaching, it is nothing less than the teaching of critical thinking.

Listening is, after all, an aggressive act. When the teacher insists that the student knows the subject and the writing process that produced the draft better than the teacher, and then has faith that the student has an other self that has monitored the producing of the draft, then the teacher puts enormous pressure on the student. Intelligent comments are expected, and when they are expected they are often received.

I have been impressed by how effectively primary students, those in the first three grades in school, have a speaking other self. Fortunately this other self that monitors the writing process has been documented on tape in a longitudinal study conducted in the Atkinson, New Hampshire, schools by Donald Graves, Lucy Calkins and Susan Sowers at the University of New Hampshire. There the other self has been recorded and analyzed.

The most effective learning takes place when the other self articulates the writing that went well. Too much instruction is failure centered. It focuses on error and unintentionally reinforces error.

The successful writer does not so much correct error as discover what is working and extend that element in the writing. The writer looks for the voice, the order, the relationship of information that is working well, and concentrates on making the entire piece of writing have the effectiveness of the successful fragment. The responsive teacher is always attempting to get the student to bypass the global evaluations of failure — "I can't write about this," "It's an airball." "I don't have anything to say." and move into an element that is working well. In the beginning of a piece of writing by a beginning student that first concern might well be the subject or the feeling that the student has toward the subject. The teacher may well say, "Okay. This draft isn't working, but what do you know about the subject that a reader needs to know?"

Again and again the teacher listens to what the student is saying — and not saying — to help the student hear that other self that has been monitoring what isn't yet on the page or what may be beginning to appear on the page.

This dialogue between the student's other self and the teacher occurs best in conference. But the conferences should be short and frequent.

"I dunno," the student says. "In reading this over I think maybe I'm more specific." The teacher scans the text and responds, "I agree. What are you going to work on next?" "I guess the ending. It sorta goes on." "Okay. Let me see it when it doesn't."

The important thing is that only one or two issues are dealt with in a conference. The conference isn't a psychiatric session. Think of the writer as an apprentice at the workbench with a master workman, a senior colleague, stopping by once in a while for a quick chat about the work.

We can also help the other self to become articulate by having the student write, after completing a draft, a brief statement about the draft. That statement can be attached on the front of the draft so the teacher can hear what the other self says and respond, after reading that statement and the draft, in writing. I have found this far less effective than the face-to-face conference, where the act of listening is personal, and where the teacher can hear the inflection and the pause as well as the statement and where the teacher can listen with the eye, reading the student's body language as well as the student's text.

The other self develops confidence through the experience of being heard in small and large group workshops. The same dynamics take place as have been modeled in the conference. The group leader asks the writer, "How can we help you?" The other self speaks of the process or of the text. The workshop members listen and read the text with the words of the other self in their ears. Then they respond, helping the other self become a more effective reader of the evolving text.

The papers that are published in workshops should be the best papers. The workshop members need to know how good writing is made, and then need to know how good writing can be improved. I always make clear that the papers being published in workshops are the best ones. As the other self speaks of how these good papers have been made and how they can be improved, the student being published has the student's most effective writing process reinforced. You can hear the other self becoming stronger and more confident as it speaks of what worked and as it proposes what may work next. The other workshop members hear an effective other self. They hear how a good writer reads an evolving draft. And during the workshop sessions their other selves start to speak, and they hear their own other selves participate in the helpful process of the workshop.

The teacher must always remember that the student, in the beginning of the course, does not know the other self exists. Its existence is an act of faith for the teacher. Sometimes that is a stupendous act of faith. Ronald, his nose running, his prose stalled, does not appear to have a self, and certainly not a critical, constructive other self. But even Ronald will hear that intelligent other self if the teacher listens well.

The teacher asks questions for which the student does not think there are answers: Why did you use such a strong word here? How did you cut this description and make it clearer? Why did you add so many specifics on Page 39? I think this ending really works, but what did you see that made you realize that old beginning was the new ending?

The student has the answers. And the student is surprised by the fact of answers as much as the answers themselves. The teacher addresses a self that the student didn't know exists, and the

student listens with astonishment to what the other self is saying —
"Hey, he's not so dumb." "That's pretty good, she knows what
she's doing."

The teacher helps the student find the other self, get to know the
other self, learn to work with the other self, and then the teacher
walks away to deal with another Ronald in another course who does
not know there is another self. The teacher's faith is building
experience. If Ronald had another self, then there is hope for faith.

What happens in the writing conference and the workshop in
which the other self is allowed to become articulate is best
expressed in the play, *The Elephant Man*, by Bernard Pomerance,
when Merrick, the freak, who has been listened to for the first time
in his life, says, "Before I spoke with people, I did not think of all
those things because there was no-one to think them for. Now
things come out of my mouth which are true."

# Writer-Based Prose:
## A Cognitive Basis for Problems in Writing

by LINDA FLOWER
*Carnegie-Mellon University*

IF WRITING IS simply the act of "expressing what you think" or "saying what you mean," why is writing often such a difficult thing to do? And why do papers that do express what the writer meant (to his or her own satisfaction) often fail to communicate the same meaning to a reader? Although we often equate writing with the straightforward act of "saying what we mean," the mental struggles writers go through and the misinterpretations readers still make suggest that we need a better model of this process. Modern communication theory and practical experience agree; writing prose that actually communicates what we mean to another person demands more than a simple act of self-expression. What communication theory does not tell us is how writers do it.

An alternative to the "think it/say it" model is to say that effective writers do not simply *express* thought but *transform* it in certain complex but describable ways for the needs of a reader. Conversely, we may find that ineffective writers are indeed merely "expressing" themselves by offering up an unretouched and underprocessed version of their own thought. Writer-Based prose, the subject of this paper, is a description of this undertransformed mode of verbal expression.

As both a style of writing and a style of thought, Writer-Based prose is natural and adequate for a writer writing to himself or herself. However, it is the source of some of the most common and pervasive problems in academic and professional writing. The symptoms can range from a mere missing referent or an underdeveloped idea to an unfocused and apparently pointless discussion. The symptoms are diverse but the source can often be traced to the writer's underlying strategy for composing and to his or her failure to transform private thought into a public, reader-based expression.

In *function*, Writer-Based prose is a verbal expression written by a writer to himself and for himself. It is the record and the working of his own verbal thought. In its *structure*, Writer-Based prose reflects the associate, narrative path of the writer's own confrontation with her subject. In its *language*, it reveals her use of privately loaded terms and shifting but unexpressed contexts for her statements.

In contrast, Reader-Based prose is a deliberate attempt to communicate something to a reader. To do that it creates a shared language and shared context between writer and reader. It also offers the reader an issue-centered rhetorical structure rather than a replay of the writer's discovery process. In its language and structure, Reader-Based prose reflects the *purpose* of the writer's thought; Writer-Based prose tends to reflect its *process*. Good writing, therefore, is often the cognitively demanding transformation of the natural but private expressions of Writer-Based thought into a structure and style adapted to a reader.

This analysis of Writer-Based prose style and the transformations that create Reader-Based prose will explore two hypotheses:

1. Writer-Based prose represents a major and familiar mode of expression which we all use from time to time. While no piece of writing is a pure example, Writer-Based prose can be identified by features of structure, function, and style. Furthermore, it shares many of these features with the modes of inner and egocentric speech described by Vygotsky and Piaget. This paper will explore that relationship and look at newer research in an effort to describe Writer-Based prose as a verbal style which in turn reflects an underlying cognitive process.

2. Writer-Based prose is a workable concept which can help us teach writing. As a way to intervene in the thinking process, it taps intuitive communication strategies writers already have, but are not adequately using. As a teaching technique, the notion of transforming one's own Writer-Based style has proved to be a powerful idea with a built-in method. It helps writers attack this demanding cognitive task with some of the thoroughness and confidence that comes from an increased and self-conscious control of the process.

My plan for this paper is to explore Writer-Based prose from a number of perspectives. Therefore, the next section, which considers the psychological theory of egocentrism and inner speech, is followed by a case study of Writer-Based prose. I will then pull these practical and theoretical issues together to define the critical features of Writer-Based prose. The final section will look ahead to the implications of this description of Writer-Based prose for writers and teachers.

INNER SPEECH AND EGOCENTRISM. In studying the developing thought of the child, Jean Piaget and Lev Vygotsky both observed a mode of speech which seemed to have little social or communicative function. Absorbed in play, children would carry on spirited elliptical monologues which they seemed to assume others understood, but which in fact made no concessions to the needs of the listener. According to Piaget, in Vygotsky's synopsis, "In egocentric speech, the child talks only about himself, takes no interest in his interlocutor, does not try to communicate, expects no answers, and often does not even care whether anyone listens to him. It is similar to a monologue in a play: The child is thinking aloud, keeping up a running accompaniment, as it were, to whatever he may be doing."[1] In the seven-year olds Piaget studied, nearly fifty percent of their recorded talk was egocentric in nature?[2] According to Piaget, the child's "non-communicative" or egocentric speech is a reflection, not of selfishness, but of the child's limited ability to "assume the point of view of the listener: [the child] talks of himself, to himself, and by himself."[3] In a sense, the child's cognitive capacity has locked her in her own monologue.

When Vygotsky observed a similar phenomenon in children he called it "inner speech" because he saw it as a forerunner of the private verbal thought adults carry on. Furthermore, Vygotsky argued, this speech is not simply a by-product of play, it is the tool children use to plan, organize, and control their activities. He put the case quite strongly: "We have seen that egocentric speech is not suspended in a void but is directly related to the child's practical dealings with the real world . . . it enters as a constituent part into the process of rational activity" (*Thought and Language*, p. 22).

The egocentric talk of the child and the mental, inner speech of the adult share three important features in common. First, they are highly elliptical. In talking to oneself the psychological subject of discourse (the old information to which we are adding new predicated) is always known. Therefore, explicit subjects and referents disappear. Five people straining to glimpse the bus need only say, "Coming!" Secondly, inner speech frequently deals in the sense of words, not their more specific or limited public meanings. Words become "saturated with sense" in much the way a key word in a poem can come to represent its entire, complex web of meaning. But unlike the word in the poem, the accrued sense of the word in inner speech may be quite personal, even idiosyncratic; it is, as Vygotsky writes, "the sum of all the psychological events aroused in our consciousness by the word" (*Thought and Language*, p. 146).

Finally, a third feature of egocentric/inner speech is the absence of logical and causal relations. In experiments with children's use of logical-causal connectives such as *because, therefore,* and *although,* Piaget found that children have difficulty managing such relationships and in spontaneous speech will substitute a non-logical, non-causal connective such as *then.* Piaget described this strategy for relating things as *juxtaposition:* "the cognitive tendency simply to link (juxtapose) one thought element to another, rather than to tie them together by some causal or logical relation."[4]

One way to diagnose this problem with sophisticated relationships is to say, as Vygotsky did, that young children often think in *complexes* instead of concepts.[5] When people think in complexes they unite objects into families that really do share common bonds, but the bonds are concrete and factual rather than abstract or logical. For example, the notion of "college student" would be a complex if it were based, for the thinker, on facts such as college students live in dorms, go to classes, and do homework.

Complexes are very functional formations, and it may be that many people do most of their day-to-day thinking without feeling the need to form more demanding complex concepts. *Complexes* collect related objects; *concepts,* however, must express abstract, logical relations. And it is just this sort of abstract, synthetic thinking that writing typically demands. In a child's early years the ability to form complex concepts may depend mostly on developing cognitive capacity. In adults this ability appears also to be a skill developed by training and a tendency fostered by one's background and intellectual experience. But whatever its source, the ability to move from the complexes of egocentric speech to the more formal relations of conceptual thought is critical to most expository writing.

Piaget and Vygotsky disagreed on the source, exact function, and teleology of egocentric speech, but they did agree on the features of this distinctive phenomenon, which they felt revealed the underlying logic of the child's thought. For our case, that may be enough. The hypothesis on which this paper rests is not a developmental one. Egocentric speech, or rather its adult written analogue, Writer-Based prose, is not necessarily a stage through which a writer must develop or one at which some writers are arrested. But for adults it does represent an available mode of expression on which to fall back. If Vygotsky is right, it may even be closely related to normal verbal thought. It is clearly a natural, less cognitively demanding mode of thought and one which explains why people, who can express themselves in complex and highly intelligible modes, are often obscure. Egocentric expression happens to the best of us; it comes naturally.

The work of Piaget and Vygotsky, then, suggests a source for the cognitive patterns that underlie Writer-Based prose, and it points to some of the major features such a prose style would possess. Let us now turn to a more detailed analysis of such writing as a verbal style inadequately suited for the needs of the reader.

WRITER-BASED PROSE: A CASE STUDY OF A TRANSFORMATION. As an introduction to the main features of Writer-Based prose and its transformations, let us look at two drafts of a progress report written by students in an organizational psychology class. Working as consulting analysts to a local organization, the writers needed to show progress to their instructor and to present an analysis with causes and conclusions to the client. Both readers — academic and professional — were less concerned with what the students did or saw than with *why* they did it and *what* they made of their observations.

To gauge the Reader-Based effectiveness of this report, skim quickly over Draft 1 and imagine the response of the instructor of the course, who needed to answer these questions: As analysts, what assumptions and decisions did my students make? Why did they make them? At what stage in the project are they now? Or, play the role of the client-reader who wants to know: How did they define my problem, and what did they conclude? As either reader, can you quickly extract the information the report should be giving you? Next, try the same test on Draft 2.

DRAFT 1:
GROUP REPORT

(1) Work began on our project with the initial group decision to evaluate the Oskaloosa Brewing Company. Oskaloosa Brewing Company is a regionally located brewery manufacturing several different types of beer, notably River City and Brough Cream Ale. This beer is marketed under various names in Pennsylvania and other neighboring states. As a group, we decided to analyze this organization because two of our group members had had frequent customer contact with the sales department. Also, we were aware that Oskaloosa Brewing had been losing money for the past five years and we felt we might be able to find some obvious problems in their organizational structure.

(2) Our first meeting, held February 17th, was with the head of the sales department, Jim Tucker. Generally, he gave us an outline of the organization from president to worker, and discussed the various departments that we might ultimately decide to analyze. The two that seemed the most promising and most applicable to the project were the sales and production departments. After a few group meetings and discussions with the personnel manager, Susan Harris, and our advisor Professor Charns, we felt it best suited our needs and the Oskaloosa Brewing's to evaluate their bottling department.

(3) During the next week we had a discussion with the superintendent of production, Henry Holt, and made plans for interviewing the supervisors and line workers. Also, we had a tour of the bottling department which gave us a first hand look into the production process. Before beginning our interviewing, our group met several times to formulate appropriate questions to use in interviewing, for both the supervisors and workers. We also had a meeting with Professor Charns to discuss this matter.

(3a) The next step was the actual interviewing process. During the weeks of March 14-18 and March 21-25, our group met several times at Oskaloosa Brewing and interviewed ten supervisors and twelve workers. Finally during this past week, we have had several group meetings to discuss our findings and the potential problem areas within the bottling department. Also, we have spent time organizing the writing of our progress report.

(4) The bottling and packaging division is located in a separate building, adjacent to the brewery, where the beer is actually manufactured. From the brewery the beer is piped into one of five lines (four bottling lines and one canning line), in the bottling house where the bottles are filled, crowned, pasteurized, labeled, packaged in cases, and either shipped out or stored in the warehouse. The head of this operation, and others, is production manager, Phil Smith. Next in line under him in direct control of the bottling house is the superintendent of bottling and packaging, Henry Holt. In addition, there are a total of ten supervisors who report directly to Henry Holt and who oversee the daily operations and coordinate and direct the twenty to thirty union workers who operate the lines.

(5) During production, each supervisor fills out a data sheet to explain what was actually produced during each hour. This form also includes the exact time when a breakdown occurred, what it was caused by, and when production was resumed. Some supervisors' positions are production staff oriented. One takes care of supplying the raw material (bottles, caps, labels, and boxes) for production. Another is responsible for the union workers assignment each day.

These workers are not all permanently assigned to a production line position. Men called "floaters" are used filling in for a sick worker, or helping out after a breakdown.

(6) The union employees are generally older than 35, some in their late fifties. Most have been with the company many years and are accustomed to having more workers per a slower moving line. They are resentful to what they declare "unnecessary" production changes. Oskaloosa Brewery also employs mechanics who normally work on the production line, and assume a mechanics job only when a breakdown occurs. Most of these men are not skilled.

## DRAFT 2:
### MEMORANDUM

TO:     Professor Martin Charns

FROM:  Nancy Lowenberg, Todd Scott, Rosemary Nisson, Larry Vollen

DATE:  March 31, 1977

RE:     *Progress Report: The Oskaloosa Brewing Company*

### WHY OSKALOOSA BREWING?

(1) Oskaloosa Brewing Company is a regionally located brewery manufacturing several different types of beer, notably River City and Brough Cream Ale. As a group, we decided to analyze this organization because two of our group members have frequent contact with the sales department. Also, we were aware that Oskaloosa Brewing had been losing money for the past five years and we felt we might be able to find some obvious problems in their organizational structure.

### INITIAL STEPS: WHERE TO CONCENTRATE?

(2) Through several interviews with top management and group discussion, we felt it best suited our needs, and Oskaloosa Brewing's, to evaluate the production department. Our first meeting, held February 17, was with the head of the sales department, Jim Tucker. He gave us an outline of the organization and described the two major departments, sales and production. He indicated that there were more obvious problems in the production department, a belief also implied by Susan Harris, personnel manager.

### NEXT STEP

(3) The next step involved a familiarization of the plant and its employees. First, we toured the plant to gain an understanding of the brewing and bottling process. Next, during the weeks of March

14-18 and March 21-25, we interviewed ten supervisors and twelve workers. Finally, during the past week we had group meetings to exchange information and discuss potential problems.

## THE PRODUCTION PROCESS

(4) Knowledge of the actual production process is imperative in understanding the effects of various problems on efficient production; therefore, we have included a bried summary of this process.

The bottling and packaging division is located in a separate building, adjacent to the brewery, where the beer is actually manufactured. From the brewery the beer is piped into one of five lines (four bottling lines and one canning line) in the bottling house where the bottles are filled, crowned, pasteurized, labeled, packaged in cases, and either shipped out or stored in the warehouse.

## PEOPLE BEHIND THE PROCESS

(5) The head of this operation is production manager, Phil Smith. Next in line under him in direct control of the bottling house is the superintendent of bottling and packaging, Henry Holt. He has authority over ten supervisors who each have two major responsibilities: (1) to fill out production data sheets that show the amount produced/hour, and information about any breakdowns — time, cause, etc., and (2) to oversee the daily operations and coordinate and direct the twenty to thirty union workers who operate the lines. These workers are not all permanently assigned to a production line position. Men called "floaters" are used to fill in for a sick worker or to help out after a breakdown.

(6) The union employees are highly diversified group in both age and experience. They are generally older than 35, some in their late fifties. Most have been with the company many years and are accustomed to having more workers per a slower moving line. They are resentful to what they feel are unnecessary production changes. Oskaloosa Brewing also employs mechanics who normally work on the production line, and assume a mechanics job only when a breakdown occurs. Most of these men are not skilled.

## PROBLEMS

Through extensive interviews with supervisors and union employees, we have recognized four apparent problems within the bottle house operations. First, the employees' goals do not match those of the company. This is especially apparent in the union employees whose loyalty lies with the union instead of the company. This attitude is well-founded as the union ensures them of job security and benefits. . . .

In its tedious misdirection, Draft 1 is typical of Writer-Based prose in student papers and professional reports. The reader is forced to do most of the thinking, sorting the wheat from the chaff and drawing ideas out of details. And yet, although this presentation fails to fulfill our needs, it does have an inner logic of its own. The logic which organizes Writer-Based prose often rests on three principles: its underlying focus is egocentric, and it uses either a narrative framework or a survey form to order ideas.

The *narrative framework* of this discussion is established by the opening announcement: "Work began. . . ." In paragraphs 1-3 facts and ideas are presented in terms of when they were discovered, rather than in terms of their implications or logical connections. The writers recount what happened when; the reader, on the other hand, asks, "Why?" and "So what?" Whether he or she likes it or not the reader is in for a blow-by-blow account of the writers' discovery process.

Although a rudimentary chronology is reasonable for a progress report, a narrative framework is often a substitute for analytic thinking. By burying ideas within the events that precipitated them, a narrative obscures the more important logical and hierarchical relations between ideas. Of course, such a narrative could read like an intellectual detective story, because, like other forms of drama, it creates interest by withholding closure. Unfortunately, most academic and professional readers seem unwilling to sit through these home movies of the writer's mind at work. Narratives can also operate as a cognitive "frame" which itself generates ideas[6]. The temporal pattern, once invoked, opens up a series of empty slots waiting to be filled with the details of what happened next, even though those details may be irrelevant. As the revision of Draft 2 shows, our writers' initial narrative framework led them to generate a shaggy project story, instead of a streamlined logical analysis.

The second salient feature of this prose is its focus on the discovery process of the writers: the "I did/I thought/I felt" focus. Of the fourteen sentences in the first three paragraphs, ten are grammatically focused on the writers' thoughts and actions rather than on issues: "Work began," "We decided," "Also we were aware . . . and we felt. . . ."

In the fourth paragraph the writers shift attention from their discovery process to the facts discovered. In doing so they illustrate a third feature of Writer-Based prose: its idea structure simply copies the structure of the perceived information. A problem arises when the internal structure of the data is not already adapted to the needs of the reader or the intentions of the writer. Paragraph five, for example, appears to be a free-floating description of "What happens during production." Yet the client-reader already knows this and the instructor probably does not care. Lured by the fascination of facts, these writer-based writers recite a litany of perceived information under the illusion they have produced a rhetorical structure. The resulting structure could as well be a neat hierarchy as a list. The point is that the writers' organizing principle is dictated by their information, not by their intention.

The second version of this report is not so much a "rewrite" (i.e., a new report) as it is a transformation of the old one. The writers had to step back from their experience and information in order to turn facts into concepts. Pinpointing the telling details was not enough: they had to articulate the meaning they saw in the data. Secondly, the writers had to build a rhetorical structure which acknowledged the function these ideas had for their reader. In the second version, the headings, topic sentences, and even some of the subjects and verbs reflect a new functional structure focused on Process, People, and Problems. The report offers a hierarchical organization of the facts in which the hierarchy itself is based on issues both writer and reader agree are important. I think it likely that such transformations frequently go on in the early stages of the composing process for skilled writers. But for some writers the under-transformed Writer-Based prose of Draft 1 is also the final product and the starting point for our work as teachers.

In the remainder of this paper I will look at the features of Writer-Based prose and the ways it functions for the writer. Clearly, we need to know about Reader-Based prose in order to teach it. But it is also clear that writers already possess a great deal of intuitive knowledge about writing for audiences when they are stimulated to use it. As the case study shows, the concept of trying to transform Writer-Based prose for a reader is by itself a powerful tool. It helps writers identify the lineaments of a problem many can start to solve once they recognize it as a definable problem.

WRITER-BASED PROSE: FUNCTION, STRUCTURE, AND STYLE. While Writer-Based prose may be inadequately structured for a reader, it does possess a logic and structure of its own. Furthermore, that structure serves some important functions for the writer in his or her effort to think about a subject. It represents a practical strategy for dealing with information. If we could see Writer-Based prose as a *functional system* — not a set of random errors known only to English teachers — we would be better able to teach writing as a part of any discipline that asks people to express complex ideas.

According to Vygotsky, "the inner speech of the adult represents his 'thinking for himself' rather than social adaptation [communication to others]: i.e., it has the same function that egocentric speech has in the child" (*Language and Thought*, p. 18). It helps him solve problems. Vygotsky found that when a child who is trying to draw, encounters an obstacle (no pencils) or a problem (what shall I call it?), the incidence of egocentric speech can double.

If we look at an analogous situation — an adult caught up in the complex mental process of composing — we can see that much of the adult's output is not well adapted for public consumption either. In studies of cognitive processes of writers as they composed, J. R. Hayes and I observed much of the writer's verbal output to be an attempt to manipulate stored information into some acceptable pattern of meaning? To do that, the writer generates a variety of alternative relationships and trial formulations of the information she has in mind. Many of these trial networks will be discarded; most will be significantly altered through recombination and elaboration during the composing process. In those cases in which the writer's first pass at articulating knowledge was also the final draft — when she wrote it just as she thought it — the result was often a series of semi-independent, juxtaposed networks, each with its own focus.

Whether such expression occurs in an experimental protocol or a written draft, it reflects the working of the writer's mind upon his material. Because dealing with one's material is a formidable enough task in itself, a writer may allow himself to ignore the additional problem of accommodating a reader. Writer-Based prose, then, functions as a medium for thinking. It offers the writer the luxury of one less constraint. As we shall see, its typical structure and style are simply paths left by the movement of the writer's mind.

The *structure* of Writer-Based prose reflects an economical strategy we have for coping with information. Readers generally expect writers to produce complex concepts — to collect data and details under larger guiding ideas and place those ideas in an integrated network. But as both Vygotsky and Piaget observed, forming such complex concepts is a demanding cognitive task; if no one minds, it is a lot easier to just list the parts. Nor is it surprising that in children two of the hallmarks of egocentric speech are the absence of expressed causal relations and the tendency to express ideas without proof or development. Adults too avoid the task of building complex concepts buttressed by development and proof, by structuring their information in two distinctive ways: as a narrative of their own discovery process or as a survey of the data before them.

As we saw in the Oskaloosa Brewing Case Study, a *narrative* ✓ structured around one's own discovery process may seem the most natural way to write. For this reason it can sometimes be the best way as well, if a writer is trying to express a complex network of information but is not yet sure how all the parts are related. For example, my notes show that early fragments of this paper started out with a narrative, list-like structure focused on my own experience: "Writer-Based prose is a working hypothesis because it works in the classroom. In fact, when I first started teaching the concept. . . . In fact, it was my students' intuitive recognition of the difference between Writer-Based and Reader-Based style in their own thought and writing. . . . It was their ability to use even a sketchy version of the distinction to transform their own writing that led me to pursue the idea more thoroughly."

The final version of this sketch keeps the reference to teaching experience, but subordinates it to the more central issue of why the concept works. This transformation illustrates how a writer's major propositions can, on first appearance, emerge embedded in a narrative of the events or thoughts which spawned the proposition. In this example, the Writer-Based early version recorded the raw material of observations; the final draft formed them into concepts and conclusions.

This transformation process may take place regularly when a writer is trying to express complicated information which is not yet fully conceptualized. Although much of this mental work normally precedes actual writing, a first draft may simply reflect the writer's current place in the process. When this happens rewriting and editing are vital operations. Far from being a simple matter of correcting errors, editing a first draft is often the act of transforming a narrative network of information into a more fully hierarchical set of propositions.

A second source of pre-fabricated structure for writers is the internal structure of the information itself. Writers use a *survey* strategy to compose because it is a powerful procedure for retrieving and organizing information. Unfortunately, the original organization of the data itself (e.g., the production process at Oskaloosa Brewing) rarely fits the most effective plan for any given piece of focused analytical writing.

The prose that results from such a survey can, of course, take as many forms as the data. It can range from a highly structured piece of discourse (the writer repeats a textbook exposition) to an unfocused printout of the writer's memories and thoughts on the subject. The form is merely a symptom, because the governing force is the writer's mental strategy: namely, to compose by surveying the available contents of memory without adapting them to a current purpose. The internal structure of the data dictates the rhetorical structure of the discourse, much as the proceedings of Congress organize the *Congressional Record*. As an information processor, the writer is performing what computer scientists would call a "memory dump": dutifully printing out memory in exactly the form in which it is stored.

A survey strategy offers the writer a useful way into the composing process in two ways. First, it eliminates many of the constraints normally imposed by a speech act, particularly the contract between reader and writer for mutually useful discourse. Secondly, a survey of one's own stored knowledge, marching along like a textbook or flowing with the tide of association, is far easier to write than a fresh or refocused conceptualization would be.

But clearly most of the advantages here accrue to the writer. One of the tacit assumptions of the Writer-Based writer is that, once the relevant information is presented, the reader will then do the work of abstracting the essential features, building a conceptual hierarchy, and transforming the whole discussion into a functional network of ideas.

Although Writer-Based prose often fails for readers and tends to preclude further concept formation, it may be a useful road into the creative process for some writers. The structures which fail to work for readers may be powerful strategies for retrieving information from memory and for exploring one's own knowledge network. This is illustrated in Linde and Labov's well-known New York apartment tour experiment? Interested in the strategies people use for retrieving information from memory and planning a discourse, Linde and Labov asked one hundred New Yorkers to "tell me the layout of your apartment" as a part of a "sociological survey." Only 3% of the subject responded with a map which gave an overview and then filled in the details; for example, "I'd say it's laid out in a huge square pattern, broken down into 4 units." The overwhelming majority (97%) all solved the problem by describing a tour: "You walk in the front door. There was a narrow hallway. To the left, etc." Furthermore, they had a common set of rules for how to conduct the tour (e.g., you don't "walk into" a small room with no outlet, such as a pantry; you just say, "on the left is . . ."). Clearly the tour structure is so widely used because it is a remarkably efficient strategy for recovering all of the relevant information about one's apartment, yet without repeating any of it. For example, one rule for "touring" is that when you dead-end after walking through two rooms, you don't "walk" back but suddenly appear back in the hall.

For us, the revealing sidenote to this experiment is that although the tour strategy was intuitively selected by the overwhelming majority of the speakers, the resulting description was generally very difficult for the listener to follow and almost impossible to reproduce. The tour strategy — like the narrative and textbook structure in prose — is a masterful method for searching memory but a dud for communicating that information to anyone else.

Finally, the *style* of Writer-Based prose also has its own logic. Its two main stylistic features grow out of the private nature of interior monologue, that is, of writing which is primarily a record or expression of the writer's flow of thought. The first feature is that in such monologues the organization of sentences and paragraphs reflects the shifting focus of the writer's attention. However, the psychological subject on which the writer is focused may not be reflected in the grammatical subject of the sentence or made explicit in the discussion at all. Secondly, the writer may depend on code words to carry his or her meaning. That is, the language may be "saturated with sense" and able to evoke — for the writer — a complex but unexpressed context.

Writers of formal written discourse have two goals for style which we can usefully distinguish from one another. One goal might be described as stylistic control, that is, the ability to choose a more embedded or more elegant transformation from variations which are roughly equivalent in meaning. The second goal is to create a completely autonomous text, that is, a text that does not need context, gestures, or audible effects to convey its meaning.

It is easy to see how the limits of short-term memory can affect a writer's stylistic control. For an inexperienced writer, the complex transformation of a periodic sentence — which would require remembering and relating a variety of elements and optional structures such as this sentence contains — can be a difficult juggling act. After all, the ability to form parallel constructions is not innate. Yet with practice many of these skills can become more automatic and require less conscious attention.

The second goal of formal written discourse — the complete autonomy of the text — leads to even more complex problems. According to David Olson the history of written language has been the progressive creation of an instrument which could convey complete and explicit meanings in a text. The history of writing is the transformation of language from utterance to text — from oral meaning created within a shared context of a speaker and listener to a written meaning fully represented in an autonomous text[9]

In contrast to this goal of autonomy, Writer-Based prose is writing whose meaning is still to an important degree in the writer's head. The culprit here is often the unstated psychological subject. The work of the "remedial" student is a good place to examine the phenomenon because it often reveals first thoughts more clearly than the reworked prose of a more experienced writer who edits as he or she writes. In the most imaginative, comprehensive and practical book to be written on the basic writer, Mina Shaughnessy has studied the linguistic strategies which lie behind the "errors" of many otherwise able young adults who have failed to master the written code. As we might predict, the ambiguous referent is ubiquitous in basic writing: *he's, she's* and *it's* are sprinkled through the prose without visible means of support. *It* frequently works as a code word for the subject the writer had in mind but not on the page. As Professor Shaughnessy says, *it* "frequently becomes a free-floating substitute for thoughts that the writer neglects to articulate and that the reader must usually strain to reach if he can."[10]

> With all the jobs available, he will have to know more of *it* because
> there is a great demand for *it*.

For the writer of the above sentence, the pronoun was probably not ambiguous at all; *it* no doubt referred to the psychological subject of his sentence. Psychologically, the subject of an utterance is the old information, the object you are looking at, the idea on which your attention has been focused. The predicate is the new information you are adding. This means that the psychological subject and grammatical subject of a sentence may not be the same at all. In our example, "college knowledge" was the writer's psychological subject — the topic he had been thinking about. The sentence itself is simply a psychological predicate. The pronoun *it* refers quite reasonably to the unstated but obvious subject in the writer's mind.

The subject is even more likely to be missing when a sentence refers to the writer herself or to "one" in her position. In the following examples, again from *Errors and Expectations*, the "unnecessary" subject is a person (like the writer) who has a chance to go to college.

> Even if a person graduated from high school who is going on to college to obtain a specific position in his career [     ] should first know how much in demand his possible future job really is.
>
> [he]

> If he doesn't because the U.S. Labor Department say's their wouldn't be enough jobs opened, [     ] is a waste to society and a "cop-out" to humanity.
>
> [he]

Unstated subjects can produce a variety of minor problems from ambiguous referents to amusing dangling modifiers (e.g., "driving around the mountain, a bear came into view"). Although prescriptive stylists are quite hard on such "errors," they are often cleared up by context or common sense. However, the controlling but unstated presence of a psychological subject can lead to some stylistic "errors" that do seriously disrupt communication. Sentence fragments are a good example.

One feature of an explicit, fully autonomous text is that the grammatical subject is usually a precise entity, often a word. By contrast, the psychological subject to which a writer wished to refer may be a complex event or entire network of information. Here written language is often rather intransigent; it is hard to refer to an entire clause or discussion unless one can produce a summary noun. Grammar, for example, normally forces us to select a specific referent for a pronoun or modifier: it wants referents and relations spelled out.[11] This specificity is, of course, its strength as a vehicle for precise reasoning and abstract thought. Errors arise when a writer uses one clause to announce his topic or psychological subject and a second clause to record a psychological predicate, a response to that old information. For example:

> The jobs that are listed in the paper, I feel you need a college degree.
> The job that my mother has, I know I could never be satisfied with it.

The preceding sentences are in error because they have failed to specify the grammatical relationship between their two elements. However, for anyone from the Bronx, each statement would be perfectly effective because it fits a familiar formula. It is an example of topicalization or Y-movement and fits a conventionalized, Yiddish influenced, intonation pattern much like the one in "Spinach — you can have it!" The sentences depend heavily on certain conventions of oral speech, and insofar as they invoke those patterns for the reader, they communicate effectively.[12]

However, most fragments do not succeed for the reader. And they fail, ironically enough, for the same reason — they too invoke intonation patterns in the reader which turn out to be misleading. The lack of punctuation gives off incorrect cues about how to segment the sentence. Set off on an incorrect intonation pattern, the thwarted reader must stop, reread and reinterpret the sentence. The following examples are from Maxine Hairston's *A Contemporary Rhetoric* (Boston: Houghton Mifflin, 1974):

> The authorities did not approve of their acts. These acts being considered detrimental to society. (society, they . . .)

> Young people need to be on their own. To show their parents that they are reliable. (reliable, young people . . .)

> (p. 322)

Fragments are easy to avoid; they require only minimal tinkering to correct. Then why is the error so persistent? One possible reason is that for the writer the fragment is a fresh predicate intented to modify the entire preceding psychological subject. The writer wants to carry out a verbal trick easily managed in speech. For the reader, however, this minor grammatical oversight is significant. It sets up and violates both intonation patterns and strong structural expectations, such as those in the last example where we expect a pause and a noun phrase to follow "reliable." The fragment, which actually refers backward, is posing as an introductory clause.

The problem with fragments is that they are perfectly adequate for the writer. In speech they may even be an effective way to express a new idea which is predicated on the entire preceding unit thought. But in a written text, fragments are errors because they do not take the needs of the reader into consideration. Looked at this way, the "goodness" of a stylistic technique or grammatical rule such as parallelism, clear antecedents, or agreement is that it is geared to the habits, expectations, and needs of the reader as well as to the demands of textual autonomy.

Vygotsky noticed how the language of children and inner speech was often "saturated with sense." Similarly, the words a writer chooses can also operate as code words, condensing a wealth of meaning in an apparently innocuous word. The following examples come from an exercise which asks writers to identify and transform some of their own pieces of mental shorthand.

The students were asked to circle any code words or loaded expressions they found in their first drafts of a summer internship application. That is, they tried to identify those expressions that might convey only a general or vague meaning to a reader, but which represented a large body of facts, experiences, or ideas for them. They then treated this code word as one would any intuition — pushing it for its buried connections and turning those into a communicable idea. The results are not unlike those brilliant explications one often hears from students who tell you what their paper really meant. This example also shows how much detailed and perceptive thought can be lying behind a vague and conventional word:

> First Draft: "By having these two jobs, I was able to see the business in an entirely different perspective." (Circle indicates a loaded expression marked by the writer.)

> Second Draft with explanation of what she actually had in mind in using the circles phrase: "By having these two jobs, I was able to see the true relationship and relative importance of the various departments in the company. I could see their mutual dependence and how an event in one part of the firm can have an important effect on another."

The tendency to think in code words is a fact of life for the writer. Yet the following example shows how much work can go into exploring our own saturated language. Like any intuition, such language is only a source of potential meanings, much as Aristotle's topics are places for finding potential arguments. In this intended example, the writer first explores her expression itself, laying out all the thoughts which were loosely connected under its name. This process of pushing our own language to give up its buried meanings forces us to make these loose connections explicit and, in the process, allows us to examine them critically. For the writer in our example, pushing her own key words leads to an important set of new ideas in the paper.

Excerpt from an application for the
National Institute of Health Internship Program

First Draft: "I want a career that will help other people while at the same time be challenging scientifically. I had the opportunity to do a biochemical assay for a neuropsychophamocologist at X-Clinic in Chicago. Besides learning the scientific procedures and techniques that are used, I realized some of the (organizational, financial and people) problems which are encountered in research. This internship program would let me pursue further my interest in research, while concurrently exposing me to (relevant and diverse) areas of bioengineering."

Excerpts from Writer's Notes Working on the Circled Phrases

Brainstorm

How did research of Sleep Center tie into overall program of X-Clinic? Not everyone within dept. knew what the others were doing, could not see overall picture of efforts.

Dr. O. — dept. head — trained for lab yet did 38-40 hrs. paperwork. Couldn't set up test assay in Sleep Center because needed equip. from biochem.

Difficulties in getting equipment

1. Politics between administrators
   Photometer at U. of ____ even though Clinic had bought it.
2. Ordering time, not sufficient inventory, had to hunt through boxes for chemicals.
3. Had to schedule use by personal contact on borrowing equipment — done at time of use and no previous planning.

No definite guidelines had been given to biochem. people as to what was "going on" with assay. Partner who was supposed to learn assay was on vacation. Two people were learning, one was on vac.

No money from state for equipment or research grants.
Departments stealing from each other.
Lobbying, politics, included.

My supervisor from India, felt prejudices on job. Couldn't advance, told me life story and difficulties in obtaining jobs at Univ. Not interested in research at Clinic per se, looking for better opportunities, studying for Vet boards.

Revision (additions in italics)

"As a biomedical researcher, I would fulfill my goal of a career that will help other people while at the same time be challenging scientifically. I had exposure to research while doing a biochemical assay for a neuropsychopharmocologist at X-Clinic in Chicago. Besides learning the scientific procedures and techniques that are used, I realized some of the organizational, financial and people problems which are encountered in research. *These problems included a lack of funds and equipment, disagreements among research staff, and the extensive amounts of time, paperwork and steps required for testing a hypothesis which was only one very small but necessary part of the overall project. But besides knowing some of the frustrations, I also know that many medical advancements, such as the cardiac pacemaker, artificial limbs and cures for diseases, exist and benefit many people because of the efforts of researchers.* Therefore I would like to pursue my interest in research by participating in the NIH Internship Program. The exposure to many *diverse projects, designed to better understand and improve the body's functioning, would help me to decide which areas of biomedical engineering to pursue.*"

We could sum up this analysis of style by noting two points. At times a Writer-Based prose style is simply an interior monologue in which some necessary information (such as intonation pattern or a psychological subject) is not expressed in the text. The solution to the reader's problem is relatively trivial in that it involves adding information that the writer already possesses. At other times, a style may be Writer-Based because the writer is thinking in code words at the level of intuited but unarticulated connections. Turning such saturated language into communicable ideas can require the writer to bring the entire composing process into play.

IMPLICATIONS FOR WRITERS AND TEACHERS. From an educational perspective, Writer-Based prose is one of the "problems" composition courses are designed to correct. It is a major cause of that notorious "breakdown" of communication between writer and reader. However, if we step back and look at it in the broader context of cognitive operations involved, we see that it represents a major, functional stage in the composing process and a powerful strategy well fitted to a part of the job of writing.

In the best of all possible worlds, good writers strive for Reader-Based prose from the very beginning: they retrieve and organize information within the framework of a reader/writer contract. Their top goal or initial question is not, "What do I know about physics, and in particularly the physics of wind resistance?" but, "What does a model plan builder need to know?" Many times a writer can do this. For a physics teacher this particular writing problem would be a trivial one. However, for a person ten years out of Physics 101, simply retrieving any relevant information would be a full-time processing job. The reader would simply have to wait. For the inexperienced writer, trying to put complex thought into written language may also be task enough. In that case, the reader is an extra constraint that must wait its turn. A Reader-Based strategy which includes the reader in the entire thinking process is clearly the best way to write, but it is not always possible. When it is very difficult or impossible to write for a reader from the beginning, writing and then transforming Writer-Based prose is a practical alternative which breaks this complex process down into manageable parts. When transforming is a practiced skill, it enters naturally into the pulse of the composing process as a writer's constant, steady effort to test and adapt his or her thought to a reader's needs. Transforming Writer-Based prose is, then, not only a necessary procedure for all writers at times, but a useful place to start teaching intellectually significant writing skills.

In this final section I will try to account for the parcular virtues of Writer-Based prose and suggest ways that teachers of writing — in any field — can take advantage of them. Seen in the context of memory retrieval, Writer-Based thinking appears to be a tapline to the rich sources of episodic memory. In the context of the composing process, Writer-Based prose is a way to deal with the overload that writing often imposes on short term memory. By teaching writers to use this transformation process we can foster the peculiar strengths of writer-based thought and still alert writers to the next transformation that many may simply fail to attempt.

One way to account for why Writer-Based prose seems to "come naturally" to most of us from time to time is to recognize its ties to our episodic as opposed to semantic memory. As Tulving describes it, "episodic memory is a more or less faithful record of a person's experiences." A statement drawn from episodic memory "refers to a personal experience that is remembered in its temporal-spatial relation to other such experiences. The remembered episodes are . . . autobiographical events, describable in terms of their perceptible dimension or attributes."[13]

Semantic memory, by contrast, "is the memory necessary for the use of language. It is a mental thesaurus, organized knowledge a person possesses about words and other verbal symbols, their meaning and referents, about relations among them, and about rules, formulas, and algorithms for the manipulation of these symbols, concepts, and relations." Although we know that table salt is NaCl and that motivation is a mental state, we probably do not remember learning the fact or the first time we thought of that concept. In semantic memory facts and concepts stand as the nexus for other words and symbols, but shorn of their temporal and autobiographical roots. If we explored the notion of "writing" in the semantic memory of someone we might produce a network such as this:

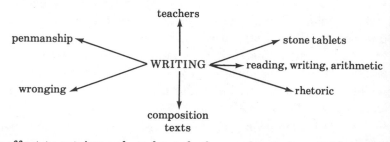

In an effort to retrieve what she or he knew about stone tablets, for example, this same person might turn to episode memory: "I once heard a lecture on the Rosetta stone, over in Maynard Hall. The woman, as I recall, said that . . . and I remember wondering if. . . ."

Writers obviously use both kinds of memory. The problem only arises when they confuse a fertile source of ideas in episodic memory with a final product. In fact, a study by Russo and Wisher argues that we sometime store our ideas or images (the symbols of thought) with the mental operations we performed to produce these symbols.[4] Furthermore, it is easier to recall the symbols (that fleeting idea, perhaps) when we bring back the original operation. In other words, our own thinking acts can serve as memory cues, and the easiest way to recover some item from memory may be to *reprocess* it, to reconstruct the original thought process in which it appeared. Much Writer-Based prose appears to be doing just this — reprocessing an earlier thinking experience as a way to recover what one knows.

Writing is one of those activities that places an enormous burden on short-term or working memory. As George Miller put it, "The most glaring result [of numerous experiments] has been to highlight man's inadequacy as a communication channel. As the amount of input information is increased, the amount of information that the man transmits increases at first but then runs into a ceiling. . . . That ceiling is always very low. Indeed, it is an act of charity to call man a channel at all. Compared to telephone or television channels, man is better characterized as a bottleneck."[15]

The short-term memory is the active central processor of the mind, that is, it is the sum of all the information we can hold in conscious attention at one time. We notice its capacity most acutely when we try to learn a new task, such as driving a car or playing bridge. Its limited capacity means that when faced with a complex problem — such as writing a college paper — we can hold and compare only a few alternative relationships in mind at once.

Trying to evaluate, elaborate, and relate all that we know on a given topic can easily overload the capacity of our working memory. Trying to compose even a single sentence can have the same effect, as we try to juggle grammatical and syntactic alternatives plus all the possibilities of tone, nuance, and rhythm even a simple sentence offers. Composing, then, is a cognitive activity that constantly threatens to overload short-term memory. For two reasons Writer-Based prose is a highly effective strategy for dealing with this problem.

1. Because the characteristic structure of Writer-Based prose is often a list (either of mental events or the features of the topic) it temporarily suspends the additional problem of forming complex concepts. If that task is suspended indefinitely, the result will fail to be good analytical writing or serious thought, but as a first stage in the process the list-structure has real value. It allows the writer freedom to generate a breadth of information and a variety of alternative relationships before locking himself or herself into a premature formulation. Furthermore, by allowing the writer to temporarily separate the two complex but somewhat different tasks of generating information and forming networks, each task may be performed more consciously and effectively.

2. Taking the perspective of another mind is also a demanding cognitive operation. It means holding not only your own knowledge network but someone else's in conscious attention and comparing them. Young children simply can't do it![16] Adults choose not to do it when their central processing is already overloaded with the effort to generate and structure their own ideas. Writer-Based prose simply eliminates this constraint by temporarily dropping the reader out of the writer's deliberations![17]

My own research suggests that good writers take advantage of these strategies in their composing process. They use scenarios, generate lists, and ignore the reader, but only for a while. Their composing process, unlike that of less effective writers, is marked by constant re-examination of their growing product and an attempt to refine, elaborate, or test its relationships, plus an attempt to anticipate the response of a reader. Everyone uses the strategies of Writer-Based prose; good writers go a step further to transform the writing these strategies produce.

But what about the writers who fail to make this transformation or (like all of us) fail to do it adequately in places? This is the problem faced by all teachers who assign papers. I think this study has two main and quite happy implications for us as teachers and writers.

The first is that Writer-Based prose is not a composite of errors or a mistake that should be scrapped. Instead, it is a half-way place for many writers and often represents the results of an extensive search and selection process. As a stage in the composing process it may be a rich compilation of significant thoughts which cohere *for the writer* into a network she or he has not yet fully articulated. Writer-Based prose is the writer's homework, and so long as the writer is also the audience, it may even be a well-thought-out communication.

The second happy implication is that writing Reader-Based prose is often simply the task of transforming the groundwork laid in the first stage of the process![18] Good analytical writing is not different in kind from the writer-based thought that seems to come naturally. It is an extension of our communication with ourselves transformed in certain predictible ways to meet the needs of the reader. The most general transformation is simply to try to take into account the reader's purpose in reading. Most people have well-developed strategies for doing this when they talk. For a variety of reasons — from cognitive effort to the illusion of the omniscient teacher/reader — many people simply do not consider the reader when they write.

More specifically, the transformations that produce Reader-Based writing include these:

Selecting a focus of mutual interest to both reader and writer (e.g., moving from the writer-based focus of "How did I go about my research or reading of the assignment and what did I see?" to a focus on "What significant conclusions can be drawn and why?").

Moving from facts, scenarios, and details to concepts.

Transforming a narrative or textbook structure into a rhetorical structure built on the logical and hierarchical relationships between ideas and organized around the purpose for writing, rather than the writer's process.

Teaching writers to recognize their own Writer-Based writing and transform it has a number of advantages. It places a strong positive value on writing that represents an effort and achievement for the writer even though it fails to communicate to the reader. This legitimate recognition of the uncommunicated content of Writer-Based prose can give anyone, but especially inexperienced writers, the confidence and motivation to go on. By defining writing as a multistage process (instead of a holistic act of "expression") we provide a rationale for editing and alert many writers to a problem they could handle once it is set apart from other problems and they deliberately set out to tackle it. By recognizing transformation as a special skill and task, we give writers a greater degree of self-conscious control over the abilities they already have and a more precise introduction to some skills they may yet develop.

## Notes:

1. Lev Vygotsky, *Thought and Language*, ed. and trans. Eugenia Hanfmann and Gertrude Vakar (Cambridge, Mass.: M.I.T. Press, 1962), p. 15.

2. Jean Piaget, *The Language and Thought of the Child*, trans. Majorie Gabin (New York: Harcourt, Brace, 1932), p. 49.

3. Herbert Ginsberg and Sylvia Opper, *Piaget's Theory of Intellectual Development* (Englewood Cliffs, N.J.: Prentice-Hall, 1969), p. 89.

4. John Flavell, *The Developmental Psychology of Jean Piaget* (New York: D. Van Nostrand, 1963), p. 275. For these studies see the last chapter of Piaget's *Language and Thought of the Child* and *Judgment and Reasoning in the Child*, trans. M. Warden (New York: Harcourt, Brace, 1926).

5. *Thought and Language*, p. 75. See also the paper by Gary Woditsch which places this question in the context of curriculum design, "Developing Generic Skills: A Model for a Competency-Based General Education," available from CUE Center, Bowling Green State University.

6. The seminal paper on frames is M. Minsky's "A Framework for Representing Knowledge" in P. Winston, ed., *The Psychology of Computer Vision* (New York: McGraw Hill, 1973). For a more recent discussion of how they work see B. Kuipers, "A Frame for Frames" in D. Bowbow and A. Collins, eds., *Representation and Understanding: Studies in Cognitive Science* (New York: Academic Press, 1975), pp. 151-184.

7. L. Flower and J. Hayes, "Plans That Guide the Composing Process," in *Writing: The Nature, Development and Teaching of Written Communication*, C. Frederikson, M. Whiteman, and J. Dominic, eds. (Hillsdale, N.J.: Lawrence Erlbaum, 1982).

8. C. Linde and W. Labov, "Spatial Networks as a Site for the Study of Language and Thought," *Language*, 51 (1975), 934-939.

9. David R. Olson, "From Utterance to Text: The Bias of Language in Speech and Writing," *Harvard Educational Review*, 47 (1977), 257-281.

10. Mina Shaughnessy, *Errors and Expectations* (New York: Oxford University Press, 1977), p. 69.

11. "Pronouns like *this, that, which* and *it* should not vaguely refer to an entire sentence or clause," and "Make a pronoun refer clearly to one antecedent, not uncertainly to two." Floyd Watkins, et al., *Practical English Handbook* (Boston: Houghton Mifflin, 1974), p. 30.

12. I am greatly indebted here to Thomas Huckin for his insightful comments on style and to his work in linguistics on how intonation patterns affect writers and readers.

13. Edel Tulving, "Episodic and Semantic Memory," in Edel Tulving and Wayne Donaldson, eds., *Organization of Memory* (New York: Academic Press, 1972), p. 387.

14. J. Russo and R. Wisher, "Reprocessing as a Recognition Cue," *Memory and Cognition*, 4 (1976), 683-689.

15. George Miller, *The Psychology of Communication* (New York: Basic Books, 1967), p. 48.

16. Marlene Scardamalia, "How Children Cope with the Cognitive Demands of Writing," in *Writing: The Nature, Development and Teaching of Written Communication*, C. Frederikson, M. Whiteman, and J. Dominic, eds. (Hillsdale, N.J.: Lawrence Erlbaum, 1982).

17. Linda Flower and John R. Hayes, "The Dynamics of Composing: Making Plans and Juggling Constraints," in *Cognitive Processes in Writing: An Interdisciplinary Approach*, Lee Gregg and Irwin Steinberg, eds. (Hillsdale, N.J.: Lawrence Erlbaum, 1979).

18. For a study of heuristics and teaching techniques for this transformation process see L. Flower and J. Hayes, "Problem-Solving Strategies and the Writing Process," *College English*, 39 (1977), 449-461.

# Writing for the Here and Now:

## An Approach to Assessing Student Writing

by STEPHEN TCHUDI
*Michigan State University*

E VALUATING STUDENT compositions has been a problem for teachers of English ever since writing became a regular part of high school English curriculums in the nineteenth century. In his textbook, *Aids to English Composition*, published in 1845, Richard Green Parker was one of the first to comment on ways of evaluating writing:

> Merits for composition should be predicted on their neatness, correctness, length, style, &c.; but the highest merits should be given for the production of ideas, and original sentiments and forms of expression.

Parker's approach to the problem seems quite contemporary with its emphasis on rewarding "the production of ideas" and "original sentiments" rather than dealing exclusively with neatness and mechanical correctness. However, like many presentday teachers, Parker found it *easier* to comment on mechanical matters than to wrestle with abstract and nebulous things like content and originality, and on the whole, his text showed far more concern for pointing out "deficiencies" than for rewarding "merits." For example, a theme grading guide at the end of the text dealt almost exclusively with the kinds of errors that could be indicated in the margins of a paper with "shorthand" symbols, "arbitrary marks" of the kind "used by printers in the correction of proof sheets." Parker may have been one of the first teachers in the country to recognize that it was quite impossible for him to write out comments on every student's paper and to turn to "shorthand" methods of evaluation. He may, in fact, have been one of the first to present the argument that using symbols was pedagogically justifiable because it forced students to locate their own errors.

I suspect that many of the devices and procedures that were developed for evaluating student writing in the years that followed were created less out of intellectual commitment than from desperation on the part of teachers faced with enormous stacks of papers. A flood of manuscripts certainly seems to have been part of the motivation behind the recommendations about composition teaching made by the Committee on Composition and Rhetoric, a group commissioned by the Board of Overseers of Harvard College later in the century. During the last quarter of the century the Harvard English department had developed an extensive writing program based on the principles of frequent writing practice and rigorous error correction. In Harvard's three writing courses, English "A," "B," and "C," the students were writing nightly, weekly, and "fortnightly" themes, each of which was carefully graded by an instructor, returned to the student for revision, and checked in a second time by the instructor. The Committee was astonished to learn that the English faculty was processing some thirty-eight thousand themes each year, work which the Committee members felt — quite rightly — to be "stupefying." The Committee's approach to the problem was simple; in its report of 1892 it tried to shift the burden to the schools using this explanation:

> It is obviously absurd that the College — the institution of higher education — should be called upon to turn aside from its proper functions, and devote its means and the time of its instructors to the task of imparting elementary instruction which should be given in ordinary grammar schools.

To their credit, not all teachers in elementary and secondary schools were willing to take up the burden, and many teachers during the period shrewdly pointed to the bad influences of "the home and street" as the source of the problem.

The problem was not, of course, solved at that time, and throughout the twentieth century, teachers have continued to develop new approaches for evaluating and assessing student writing. We have tried pointing out errors and allowing students to discover their own errors; we have hired lay readers to discover errors and offer advice *in absentia*; we have tried blanket red-pencil-ling and selective grey-pencilling of errors; we have emphasized the positive and tried to slip in occasional comments about the negative; and we have experimented with grading systems: single grades, double grades (solving the form/content dilemma by avoid-ing the issue), and multiple grades (the idea of the double grade carried to its logical, and quite possibly absurd, conclusion). We have even created a market for a twentieth-century improvement on Parker's proofreading symbols: a rubber stamp showing a little duckie who says "AWK!," protecting the ego of the child on whose paper it is imprinted by adding a playful touch to the revelation of his compositional awkwardness.

Despite these devices and procedures, however, student writing has not seemed to improve in corresponding ways. Research sur-veys, including the Braddock, Lloyd-Jones, Schoer *Research in Written Composition* (NCTE, 1963) and Stephen Sherwin's *Four Problems in Teaching English* (NCTE, 1969), show that experi-ments with grading and evaluation systems have never produced significantly positive results. Research techniques in the field are not sophisticated, of course, and it may be that the lack of "results" is a problem for researchers, not teachers. However, common sense and the experience of most teachers indicate that the research is accurate — that our grading and evaluation schemes, old or new, simple or sophisticated, have not lead to significant improvement in student writing.

Why hasn't evaluation worked? Obviously no clear answer to that question is available; if it were, we would have tried it and found success. However, I want to suggest that a major reason may be that from Parker's time to the present, approaches to evaluation have always been *future directed* rather than looking at writing as something for the *here and now*. Evaluation has emphasized getting students ready for "next time," instead of helping them find success now.

For example, with his talk of "merits" and "deficiencies," Parker sounds rather like a Puritan preacher trying to prepare his flock for the hereafter. Although we have softened the language to speak of "strengths" and "weaknesses," our attitude has remained much the same. Like the Harvard faculty of the late nineteenth century, we have operated on the assumption that if a student writes enough themes and receives enough evaluation, he will, sometime in the near or distant future, write *The Perfect Theme* that will be his pass through the compositional Golden Gates.

People write for many reasons: to share experiences, to help themselves understand what is happening, to record information, and to communicate ideas. Few people write simply for the sake of learning to write better "next time." When an evaluation procedure implies that all work is being done simply in preparation for more work in the future, the reality of the writing situation is destroyed. Ironically, future directed evaluation, even when it is done humanely and sensitively, may actually *inhibit* growth in writing.

I would argue that if the teacher ignores — for the moment — his hopes for future competence on the part of students and concentrates on helping his students find success with their writing here and now, he can expect to make writing a real, important experience for students, one through which both they and their writing will grow.

A friend who is in publishing once pointed out to me that magazine and book editors are not interested in teaching authors how to write better. When a manuscript arrives, an editor looks through it, comments on it, calls for some revisions, makes some changes, and suggests other modifications. All this "instruction" is simply aimed at getting out a successful publication. On the whole, the editor remains indifferent to whether or not the author's writing improves in the process. However, many authors acknowledge that the process does help them write better, and many writers depend quite heavily on their editors for advice. The "moral" here is that by concentrating on the present, the editor helps the writer find success, and when he does, he becomes, almost incidentally, a "teacher of writing," someone who also helps people do it better "next time."

I think we can escape the trap of future directed evaluation by adapting the general kind of attitude an editor takes. An editor, of course, works with adults who are reasonably accomplished writers to begin with. Because the teacher works with young people who are in the process of growing, both as people and as writers, his specific roles will be more complicated. At times the teacher should be an editor, dealing with strengths and weaknesses in papers as publication or public presentation approaches. At other times, however, he must serve in somewhat more sensitive roles; he may be a talent scout, adult respondent, interested human being, friend, or advisor. The roles will differ with the student, the circumstances, and the state of the original manuscript that the teacher receives. The teacher cannot simply treat themes as "a batch," giving every piece of writing the same basic evaluative "treatment." Rather, he needs to find ways of individualizing the kind of response he makes to student papers, rejecting the narrow role of teacher-evaluator and becoming a kind of "manuscript manager," deciding on an individual basis what needs to happen for a piece of writing to bring satisfaction to the student here and now.

I would like to block out, in some detail, an approach to assessing and responding to student writing that allows the teacher to examine compositions on an individual basis. It is an approach I have tried in both high school and college classes with students of a wide range of ability levels. While I don't present it as a "cure-all," it is a process which has helped me feel fairly comfortable about responding to student writing. It consists of a series of stages or "checkpoints" where the teacher can pause to consider alternative ways of helping students. Depending on the answers to questions at various points in the assessment process, many different things can happen to a manuscript. In every case, however, all evaluation, commentary, criticism, and response become directed toward the single aim of helping an individual student have a satisfying experience with his writing as quickly and effectively as possible.

1. *Listening for the Student's Voice.*

When a paper first comes in, I think the teacher needs to begin his assessment by trying to discover whether or not the student was involved in the writing activity. The teacher needs to ask if this is a *real* piece of writing. Can you hear the student "talking" when you read it? Is it a lively paper that reveals the student's active participation in his work? This quality in student writing is difficult to define but rather easy to detect. Many people call the quality "voice" — meaning that the paper sounds as if a unique person wrote it, not a computer or a bureaucrat. In *Children's Writing*

(Cambridge University Press, 1967), David Holbrook describes it as "sincerity" and characterizes it as a feeling of openness, liveliness, and animation. I enjoy Ken Macrorie's characterization of its *opposite* as "Engfish" and the paper written in that style as being "Engfishified" (*Uptaught*. Hayden, 1969).

In essence the teacher asks, "Is there evidence that this has been a productive, reasonably enjoyable writing experience for the student?" If the answer is "yes," it will be revealed in the tone of "aliveness" which one can sense in the language of the paper.

If the answer is negative, the teacher has reached an important decision point in the assessment process. Traditionally, when a teacher receives flat, dull, colorless writing, he blames it on the student: "You're not trying hard enough. Do it over!" I think this blame has been misplaced. No student deliberately creates lifeless writing. Making "Engfish" is dull and boring, and few people outside the Pentagon would choose to write very much of it. In a majority of cases, dull writing probably can be traced back to the teacher, the assignment, or an unfavorable classroom climate. Perhaps the assignment was poor — too complicated, too easy, irrelevant, or just plain silly. Perhaps the student doesn't trust the teacher or his classmates and is unwilling to share his ideas with them. Whatever the cause, I think the teacher needs to turn his attention to finding out what went wrong, looking as much to himself and his teaching as to the student for an explanation. The teacher can then stay awake at night, trying to figure out something else for the student to do. What *will* work for him? What are his interests? What are his skills? Can we find a project that will excite him? How can we persuade him to trust us?

But what does the teacher do with the manuscript? It seems pointless to demand revision or further work on something that was dead to begin with. I think the teacher should, therefore, respond as positively as he can to the paper, commenting on the "good" parts (without faking a response) and return the paper. Often the teacher can say quite directly, "Look, I had the feeling you didn't enjoy doing this. Am I right? Let's see if we can't come up with something else you would rather do."

Here is a paper that illustrates the problem of voice. It was written in a junior high school class in which the students were asked to write a letter of application for a job they would like to have sometime:

> Good morning Sir I would like to apply for a banking clerk. I think I am well qualified to fill the position. I have had three years of dealing with money I know how to handle money quite well. I am a very responsible man and also very dependable. I could be trusted to handle your money without your having any uncertainty about me. And as I said before since I have been handling money.
>
> My schooling is great, I have just graduate from college, and majoring in bookkeeping which deals with a lot of money.
>
> I can tell you how much money you are making or lossing. If you were to hire me you can be certain that I will do my job to the best of my ability. Yes! This is just the kind of bank that I would like to work at.
>
> I feel that it would be a privilege working for your bank.
>
> (H.) Allen Johnson

Except for a few bright spots, this letter seems to me quite lacking in voice, and I doubt that Allen profited much by doing it. Many of the phrases seem forced, unnatural, and excessively formal: "I could . . . handle your money without your having any uncertainty about me." "I feel it would be a privilege working for your bank." Occasionally Allen's real voice comes through. His exclamation, "Yes!," seems to be a victory over both The Business Letter and his own doubts about the banking business. His signature is done in playful parody of "official" looking signatures and adds an original touch. But the remainder is dull and repetitive, sounding much like a junior high school student trying to "make it" in what he imagines to be adult language.

The result is a letter which, by almost any criterion, is unsuccessful: Allen has not learned much about business letters; his letter *won't* land him a job; and his teacher must be thoroughly frustrated by almost every aspect of his writing.

What went wrong? I suspect that although the assignment seemed "reasonable" and "practical," the realities of job hunting are so far removed from the world of the junior high school student that the assignment became meaningless. Allen is simply not ready to worry about jobs (and there is no reason why he should be), so the assignment drove him into using a false, stuffy voice. In dealing with the paper I would compliment Allen on his enthusiasm and point out that he has done a good job of thinking about what a banker would want to know about a prospective employee. (He has done a skillful job of "surveying his audience," even though the topic and audience were not closely related to his current needs.) I would then turn attention to finding other projects that Allen would enjoy doing. It is conceivable that he might enjoy going to a bank to find out what actually happens there. I think it more likely, however, that the teacher could find interesting writing ideas for Allen in less academic areas, topics more typically for junior high school, writing sports stories or telling tales of the grotesque and macabre.

## 2. *Responding to Student Writing.*

One hopes that the amount of "voiceless" writing a teacher receives will be small and that early in the school year he can help each student find areas where writing is profitable and interesting. Once the teacher recognizes that a paper *has* voice, it is appropriate that he take time to respond (orally or in writing) to the student before going on to consider matters of revision or proofreading. A student has spent much time writing the paper; he needs response and reaction quickly.

"To respond" to student writing simply means to react to a paper openly and directly, as a "person" rather than as a teacher. It differs from evaluation in being a shared reaction rather than a set of future directed instructions for improvement. In responding the teacher can tell how he reacted to the paper ("I really felt the fear you described when the storm hit."); he can share similar experiences ("I remember the fight I had with my parents over taking a job when I was a sophomore."); he can indicate his own beliefs and tell about the ways in which he agrees or disagrees ("I can see your point about the way newscasters operate, but I really don't share your view of the President."). Response can move beyond direct reactions to suggest new or related directions for the student to explore ("You obviously enjoyed writing this. Have you ever read any of Edgar Allan Poe's stories?" "Have you ever made a movie? I think it might be interesting for you to try to catch the same idea on film."). It is the honest reaction of an interested, informed, literate adult, not the pedagogically directed instruction of a theme-grader.

In responding, however, the teacher differs from the ordinary reader in a very significant way: the teacher is willing to ignore all kinds of graphic, rhetorical, and syntactic problems that a regular reader might find frustrating or disagreeable. The teacher will *fight* to dig out the meaning of a page. He will puzzle over idiosyncratic spellings, ignore a 250-word run on sentence, forget about the fact that statistics and supporting evidence are missing, and struggle to uncoil long strings of identical loops that pass for handwriting. It is critical — at this point in the assessment process — that the teacher find the meaning of the paper and correspond with the student about it. Other "problems" can be taken care of at a later point in the process.

As David Holbrook has pointed out in *Children's Writing*, looking past problems to "decipher," appreciate, and enjoy student writing without having one's reaction biased by "errors" and "blights" is extremely difficult, more difficult for English teachers than for most people, since we have all our advanced degrees in linguistic flaw-detecting.

Perhaps the best model for this kind of response is the letter one would write in reply to something received from a young relative — a son, daughter, or nephew. For close relatives most of us are willing to decipher and to respond directly to meaning. Few of us would grade or evaluate letters from a relative, and not many parents would take time to question the usage in a sentence like, "I been smoking pot I like it." We would make almost unlimited efforts to find out what our young friends are saying, thinking, feeling, and doing. I think teachers should adopt the same attitude in responding to student writing.

### 3. *Public or Private?*

When a response has been recorded (or made directly to the student through conversation), the teacher needs to determine what should happen to the paper next. The question becomes, "Should this paper be published?" Should it be made public and given a wider audience than the teacher? Although we want to avoid writing that is "teacher-written," it is important for us to recall that not all writing is meant to be made public. The teacher should consider carefully whether providing an audience will produce a positive experience for the student.

Here is a paper submitted by a high school sophomore girl:

> One day me and this girl went to the store. The girl was from Chicago and she thought she was bad. She kept pointing her umbrella in my face. I told her stop but she kept pushing so I grabbed it out of her hand and stuck her with it. I felt sorry but I said no better for a person like that. Only fools fight. And when you fight you really lose whether you win or not. I believe that arguing is good because people have a way to say it without harming some one or hurting a live thing. But you can't always walk away. (You may not understand this because I haven't got the words to say it.)
>
> — C.S.

It is possible that C.S. would find it helpful to have other students read and discuss this paper, and her classmates might be able to offer some useful or supporting advice. However, this paper seems to fit an audience-category described by James Britton as writing addressed to "the teacher as trusted adult." C.S. is obviously puzzled and concerned about her behavior, and she seems to be less interested in "communicating a message" than exploring her own experience and seeking a response from someone else. She knows — or thinks she believes — that "only fools fight," and she is persuaded that people should settle disputes through argument rather than "harming someone or hurting a live thing." Yet, "You can't always walk away," and in this situation she felt committed to action. As a "trusted adult" (a role which the teacher should accept with pleasure, even if it sometimes puts him in the uncomfortable position of learning about students' problems), the teacher needs to respond directly to C.S., supporting her efforts to sort out her own beliefs and values.

For writing that is private, this point is another good place to end the assessment process. The teacher can respond to C.S. in the way described in the previous section. The paper should then be returned to her without any pedagogical comment. Although there may be some rhetorical problems with the writing, there seems to be no point in asking for revision. C.S. expressed her feelings; the teacher read, understood, and responded. That seems to be enough.

### 4. Determining a Form of "Publication."

If the teacher thinks a paper should be made public, there are many different ways he can provide students with a readership.

Some papers are best "published" by having them read aloud to the class, either by the author or the teacher. Some writing should be read to a tape recorder and made part of the class library of recorded literature. Students' work can be posted on the board, submitted to a class newspaper or magazine, sent to the school paper or magazine, run off for the class, or circulated in manuscript form. Every form of writing and each kind of publication makes particular, specialized demands on the writer.

Students should, of course, have an audience in mind while they are writing, but often the best form of publication will not be apparent until after the writing has been completed. A short, witty poem that might bring a good laugh to the class when read aloud might die when set in print. A paper that began as an essay on student-teacher relationships might merit being sent to the school paper, and if the editors won't publish it, it should be turned over to the underground paper. A play which has absorbed a student's time for several weeks surely deserves presentation, but it may work better as reader's theater or a radio play than as a full stage production. As an expert on writing forms, media, and styles, the teacher can help the students find the most productive forms of publication.

Here Roman Cirillo, an eighth-grader, writes about "How Airplanes Flies," and his paper presents some interesting publication problems:

> Few people know why or how an airplane flies. The explanation is very simple. There no mysterious mechenism or machinery to study. You don't have to take a plane apart or crawl around inside to understand why it stays in the air. You just stand off and look at it. Airplanes flies because of the shapes of its wings. The engine and propellor have very little to do with it. The pilot has nothing to do with making the plane fly. He simply controls the flight. A glider without an engine will fly in the air for hours. The biggest airlines will fly for a certain length of time with all the engine shut off. A plan flies and stay in the air because its wings are supported by the air just as water supports a fellow. Toss a flat piece of tin on a boat. Toss a flat piece of tin on a pond and it will sink at once. If you bend it through the middle and fasten the end together so its is watertight it will float.

There are obviously many rhetorical problems with this essay. It lacks clarity and it often leaves the reader somewhat confused. But, if one looks past the errors and "infelicities," "How Airplanes Flies" is an open, clever explanation of flight. The paper has a strong, clear voice; we can *hear* Roman's patient instruction to someone who is ignorant of the principles of flight: "You don't have to take a plane apart or crawl around inside to understand why it stays in the air. You just stand off and look at it." Roman is a good teacher, and his explanation of how shaping metal enables the plane to fly is skillful (even though incomplete). Roman would, no doubt, fail any test on writing analogies, similes, and metaphors; but he makes excellent use of analogy in relating how things float in an invisible substance — air — to a common phenomenon that is easily observable — a boat on water.

In its present form, however, the paper will probably not find much success with an audience. There are too many problems of clarity and too much drifting and backtracking for a reader (particularly one who *doesn't* understand flight) to stay with it for long.

Because Roman seems to have so much trouble handling the written word (one senses quite a struggle with the writing process behind this paper), I think the teacher might recommend that this project be completed as an oral "publication," particularly since Roman seems to be such a good "talker." Perhaps he can plan a demonstration for those members of the class who are interested. Drawing on his essay, he might bring in a dishpan and some foil to demonstrate the shaping and floating of materials. Perhaps he can bring in some model planes or photographs or drawings to illustrate flight. An oral presentation should be a good experience for him, and significantly enough, it will be an experience that has its origins in writing.

## 5. *Editing.*

I have tried to suggest that until writing has reached the publishing stage and the teacher and student have settled on a form of publication, there seems to be little point in offering comments about the rhetorical quality of students' writings. Up to this point, the teacher has been concerned with responding to the student in personal terms and trying to determine the most valuable route toward publication.

When the form of publication has been determined, commentary about writing becomes appropriate, and the teacher and student can begin raising questions about effectiveness, clarity, organization, style, and structure. However, I think it is important to relate this discussion to the *particular form of publication* and the *particular audience* for the paper. Publications and age levels have differing standards, and if editorial advice is to be helpful, it must be valid. Too often we impose blanket, adult, textbookish standards on student writing which will never be read with adult criteria of evaluation in mind.

For example, if a student writes *"Cowhide* is the crummiest show on t.v.,"* the teacher's initial reaction may be to point out that "crummy" is not a standard critical term, that one cannot simply declare a show crummy without supplying "reasons" and "supporting evidence." However, if the audience for the paper is a class of seventh-graders who watch *Cowhide* regularly, "crummiest" may be *just* the word; the students know what the show is like and will either agree that it is crummy or argue that "it isn't all *that* crummy." In either case, the students don't need "evidence" or "reasons"; they already know the arguments. On the other hand, if the student is writing to the network president to demand that the show be removed from the air, the teacher can be genuinely helpful by pointing out that the word is inappropriate, *not* to teach appropriateness or critical analysis, but to help insure that the student's letter will be read seriously by the president (or his secretary).

Sybil Marshall has suggested in *An Experiment in Education* (Cambridge University Press, 1966) that it is very difficult for the teacher to know what kinds of advice will and will not seem real to the students. Too often, she suggests, teachers try to force adult standards on young people, with the effect that the teacher's advice consistently comes out seeming hollow, academic, authoritarian, or just plain false. Most of us, in fact, can recall English teachers who were deliberately obtuse, "pretending" writing was unclear when in fact the only thing wrong was that it was written with school-age rather than adult clarity.

Perhaps the easiest way to avoid this problem is for the teacher to involve the students in the editorial process as much as possible. When the students ask specific questions, the teacher should, of course, respond freely. However, by asking the students to share writing with each other and to suggest how papers can be revised to become more effective with the audience the teacher can be reasonably certain that "real" questions will come up. With a little guidance and practice, students can become quite adept at providing constructive commentary for each other, and their advice will be more realistic (if less sophisticated) than the teacher's.

Here is an essay written for publication in a junior high school newspaper:

### Hippies

Hippies are people with long hair and dress with beads and flowers. They never shave. They are always marching and causing troubles. On one college they threw spikes, black widow spiders, and lead balls at the police. They burned a lot of things.

Hippies take L.S.D. and many other harmful drugs. This probably causes them to act queer.

The police have to hit them to straten them out.

— Bill Lowe

The teacher's initial reaction to this paper may be one of wanting to "straten" Bill out by pointing out that there are two sides to every issue, that he has overgeneralized about hippies, that he has chosen limited examples, that it is not the task of the police to "straten" people out. In doing so, however, the teacher would probably come off as moralistic and pedantic and certainly would not cause Bill to change his mind. (I do think that in *responding* to the paper the teacher could make clear that he disagrees, but once again, responding to writing is not the same as editing it.)

I would use the editorial conference with other students to sponsor a discussion of the paper. It *may* be that the students will debate Bill's assumptions and offer him advice on bringing both sides of the issue into his paper. On the other hand, it is equally possible that because of similarities of the students' family backgrounds, values, and the like, the editorial conference will *support* Bill's paper, accepting it without reservation. If that happens, the teacher should not dismiss the discussion of papers by students as "not working" but rather should recognize that "real" audiences don't always make the kinds of demands on a writer that the textbooks say they do. When Bill and his friends are a little older, they will be more sophisticated in their ways of analyzing such situations, particularly if the teacher has the confidence (and the patience) to give them the freedom to make their own editorial decisions now. If students are given frequent opportunities for editorial work, they almost invariably become more skilled, and in many respects more demanding, in asking for changes in writing.

### 6. *Copy Reading.*

For too long, textbook writers and composition teachers have blurred the distinction between editing (changing content and form) and proofreading (polishing up matters of spelling, mechanics, and usage). In our zeal to make students skillful writers of "standard" English, we have pounced on proofreading errors as early as the first draft, blithely pointing out problems in words and sentences which may well disappear entirely during the revision stage.

We should delay discussion of mechanical and syntactic correctness until the last possible moment in the writing process, leaving the students free to write, discuss, and revise papers without any hesitation because of uncertainty over rules of correctness. Only after the student has edited his writing into a final form that satisfies him should we open the discussion of mechanics and usage.

The debate over whether we should impose standard English on students is a complex one, involving psychology and sociology as much as English and linguistics, and I will not take it up in detail here. I am personally very reluctant to see "standard" *imposed* on kids in any way, be it done overtly or through subtle plans which claim to recognize the validity of a person's dialect while asking him to change it or to maintain alternatives to it.

However, as part of the copy reading process, I think the teacher should help the students who want it put their papers into a form which larger audiences will find acceptable. The teacher can point out to students (if they don't know it already from years of experience) that some audiences are "offended" by unclear handwriting or language that doesn't conform to certain "standards." The teacher might also note that failing to conform to some standards can create communications problems. Most kids see these ideas readily enough, and if "the quest for correctness" has not dominated the entire writing process, they are willing to participate in a polishing session to get their paper into a form that will not cost them readers.

Once again, however, it is important to note that the correctness demands of audience differ, and the teacher should not apply blanket standards of correctness or use the copy reading session to impose or teach standard English. The teacher should consider the proofreading changes which are necessary for *this* paper for *this* audience at *this* time. For instance, if the paper is simply to be read aloud or tape-recorded by the author, any discussion of spelling, punctuation, or capitalization is aimless and a waste of time; even if the paper is misspelled, illegibly written, and totally unpunctuated, the author can read it aloud, and discussing "problems" contributes nothing to his success. If, on the other hand, the paper is going to be duplicated, it is quite legitimate for the teacher to work with the student to help get the paper into audience-acceptable form. Even here, however, the teacher needs to be cautious. If "It's me" is the standard form in the spoken dialect of a class, the teacher should probably not try to present "It's I" as being appropriate. What matters is the audience, not a textbook description of "standard."

During the proofreading stage, the teacher can be quite direct in the instruction he offers. Instead of setting students adrift in handbooks or rule books or letting them "find their own errors," the teacher can work directly — as a proofreader might — showing the students the changes that need to be made. I suggest that the explanation be done this way because it takes much of the mystery out of the process and does not unduly delay the final publication.

In practice, of course, much of the copy work can be done by the students themselves. In every class there are a few kids who have — one way or another — mastered "the rules." The teacher can let these students share their enviable knowledge by setting them up as proofreading consultants for other members of the class.

## 7. *Publishing.*

The payoff. If the process has worked, the teacher will have the satisfaction of seeing the student's work well received, whether it is read to the class, printed, hung on the board, pasted in a book, or passed around the classroom. If the teacher has been a helpful editor and manuscript manager, the student will find success.

Equally important, I think, is that although this way of assessing student work is *not* future directed, it is nevertheless likely that the process *will* produce long range changes and improvements in the students' writing. When students find success with an audience, they remember the parts of the process that contributed to their success, including the advice and suggestions offered by the teacher and student-editors. In short, concentrating our efforts on present success will probably produce more change and "transfer" than traditional future oriented methods.

As I have described it, this approach to assessment may seem excessively complicated and time consuming — unrealistic for a teacher with five classes and 150 students. However I have found that with both college and high school classes it actually speeds up the assessment process and provides more free time for the teacher to take up other roles. I find, for example, that it takes me less time to write a note of personal response on a paper than to mull through and write out detailed, pedagogically oriented evaluative comments. It is much faster to offer direct editorial advice keyed to specific publishing situations than it is to puzzle over which errors one will selectively attack "this time." In addition, as a class "grows" in the course of a quarter or semester, the students take over more and more of the process. The stages become less distinct because the students become more adept at editing their own work, which is, of course, one of our traditional goals. All this creates more time for the teacher to move around the class working on a one-to-one basis with students who seek his help as a writing consultant.

I have said nothing of theme *grading* in this essay. Putting letter grades on thems is another of those future directed techniques which, like the Puritan minister's sermons, is designed to coach and coddle students toward the compositional hereafter. Grading seriously limits the teacher's ability to play any role but that of the theme evaluator. Without going into detail, I will suggest that even in schools where teachers are expected to submit a certain number of grades each marking period, there are many ways the teacher can subvert the grading system and avoid putting letter grades on student writing. There are many precedents for grading based on student recommendation, self-assessment, end-of-term conferences, raw quantity of work, and teacher-student contracts. It is important that anyone who wants to try this approach to the assessment of student writing explore alternatives to conventional grading. Only by beating the grading system can we fully use the advantages of having students write for the here and now.

# Time for Questions: Responding to Writing

*WHAT IS a writing conference?*

A writing conference is a *conversation* between teacher and student. It may be only a few seconds long — merely checking in with a student — or it may be an extended conversation that runs for several minutes. A major purpose of the writing conference is to encourage the students to examine and evaluate their own writing, to re-*see* it. For this reason, it is useful to ask questions like:

1. What do you like best about this draft? What do you like least?

2. What gave you the most trouble in writing this?

3. What kind of reaction do you want your readers to have — amusement, anger, increased understanding?

4. What surprised you when you wrote this? What came out different than you expected?

5. What is the most important thing you learned about your topic in writing this?

The classic danger in a writing conference is that the teacher talks too much. We all regularly violate the Shaker maxim — "Never miss an opportunity to keep your mouth shut." As students talk about their writing, they often discover connections, examples, and incidents that can strengthen their writing. Talking helps them "know what they know," it gives them access to information that often didn't make it onto the page.

*But doesn't the teacher have the responsibility of making suggestions and giving her reaction?*

Yes. I see the conference as a kind of trade — the teacher and student share reactions to the paper. But it is crucially important *how* the teacher shares a reaction. Suppose the teacher feels that a description of a bully in a student paper needs more detail. The teacher can say:

"You need to add more information about the bully."

or

"I was interested in the bully when he entered the room but I have trouble picturing him. What did he look like?"

Aside from being more diplomatic, the second response continues a conversation; it allows the student to talk his way to a clearer visualization of the bully.

*How do I find time to meet with my students individually?*

Most high school teachers meet too many students. One would hope that if school districts want writing taught, they might designate "writing intensive courses" and keep the number in these courses to a reasonable number — no more than 20. But until that day comes there are things that can be done.

First, something very simple. It helps if the teacher moves around the classroom, spends part of the writing period conducting "roving conferences." If the teacher is on the move, conferences are generally shorter than one-on-one conferences at the teacher's desk. I've watched teachers talk to as many as 12-15 students in a 50-minute class period when they move from desk to desk.

Teachers can be brief in their conferences if they don't try to do everything on a particular paper; a conference generally focuses on one aspect of the paper that is working and one that needs improvement. A teacher working, for example, on developing a fuller description of the bully should ignore spelling mistakes in the draft. In an early draft of a paper the teacher might read with these questions in mind:

1. Does the paper need more detail or documentation?

2. Is the paper sufficiently complex? Are important alternatives explored, important questions answered?

3. Is the paper focused? Does it seem to make one point or general impression?

4. Is the information ordered? Does one part move into the next?

5. Are there parts that can be cut because they're off the subject or uninteresting? (Beginnings, for example, can often be cut.)

These are some of the questions that can focus a first reading. As Donald Murray has noted, "(The experienced composition teacher) encourages the student to see that on most pieces of writing there is one fundamental problem that must be dealt with before the next problem can be spotted and then solved."

When the larger issues of information, focus, and order are resolved, the teacher can focus on questions of style and language conventions. A different set of questions can focus the reading:

1. Which errors are proofreading errors and which indicate that the student does not know certain usage rules?

2. Is there any pattern to the errors the writer makes? (Mina Shaughnessy's *Errors and Expectations* is an invaluable aid here.)

3. Are there sentences that can be combined? Broken into two sentences?

I've found that when teachers discipline their responses to papers, when they deal with one issue at a time and are not shuttling between trying to elicit more information and dealing with the semicolon, they are more effective and a conference is briefer. Conferences that lack this discipline can be long, aimless, and ineffective.

*How can I get students to be more effective in responding to the papers of their classmates?*

Many teachers worry that when students get together to comment on each others writing they might be too harsh and negative. In my experience students err on the side of blandness; comments are very general — "this is interesting," "I can relate to this," etc. Peter Elbow, in his books *Writing Without Teachers* and *Writing with Power*, offers a number of strategies for responding more specifically. One of the most basic is "pointing" which he describes as follows:

> Start by simply pointing to words and phrases which successfully
> penetrated your skull: perhaps they seemed loud and full of voice; or
> they seemed to have a lot of energy; or they somehow rang true,
> or they carried special conviction.

Students should also be encouraged to ask the writer questions
that can help expand or clarify what has been written. Again we're
talking about *questions* which allow the writer to expand and clarify
orally, not *judgments* passed on to the writer.

It is often easier to begin peer response by having students pair
up; there is generally no hesitancy to confer in pairs. Once groups of
4 or 5 are formed they should remain constant for at least several
weeks.

*I have to grade my students. How can I assign grades and still
maintain a workshop approach to writing?*

It's best not to grade every piece of writing. Students should be
encouraged to select their best writing from their writing folders to
be evaluated for a grade. By grading only the best work, the system
provides a real incentive for revising because it is often in the student's interest to revise a promising piece than to continually start
a new one.

At the end of a marking period a student might be evaluated as
follows. All students who complete a satisfactory volume of writing
— those who worked regularly and met deadlines — should get a
base grade, perhaps a C + . This base grade can go up if the student
has made major improvement on a skill identified at the beginning
of the marking term or if the quality of the selected pieces of writing
is superior.

This system rewards productivity; a student who writes several
thousand words in a marking term does not, in my opinion, deserve
a D, even if there are substantial difficulties in that writing. The
system also rewards quality; excellent writing gets an excellent
grade. The system penalizes sloth — and that's the way it should be.

# Suggestions for Further Reading:
## Responding to Writing

Atwell, Nancie. "Making the Grade: Evaluating Writing in Conference" in Thomas Newkirk and Nancie Atwell, editors, *Understanding Writing: Ways of Observing, Learning, and Teaching* (Chelmsford, Massachusetts: Northeast Regional Exchange, 1982).

Carnicelli, Thomas. "The Writing Conference: A One-to-One Conversation" in Timothy Donovan and Benjamin McClelland, editors, *Eight Approaches to Teaching Composition* (Urbana, Illinois: National Council of Teachers of English, 1980).

Cooper, Charles and Lee Odell. *Evaluating Writing: Describing, Measuring, and Judging* (Urbana, Illinois: National Council of Teachers of English, 1977).

Elbow, Peter. *Writing with Power: Techniques for Mastering the Writing Process* (New York: Oxford University Press, 1981. See especially his chapters on "reader-based" and "criterion-based" feedback.

Elbow, Peter. *Writing Without Teachers* (New York: Oxford University Press, 1973).

Halley, Hasse. "The Bundle," in Thomas Newkirk and Nancie Atwell, editors, *Understanding Writing: Ways of Observing, Learning, and Teaching* (Chelmsford, Massachusetts: Northeast Regional Exchange, 1982).

Kirby, Dan and Tom Liner. "Revision: Yes, They Do It," *English Journal*, (March, 1980): 41-45.

Knoblauch, Cy and Lil Brannon. *Rhetorical Traditions and the Teaching of Writing* (Montclair, New Jersey: Boynton/Cook, 1984). See especially the chapter, "Responding to Texts."

Murray, Donald. "The Listening Eye: Reflections on the Writing Conference" in his *Learning by Teaching* (Montclair, New Jersey: Boynton/Cook Publishers, 1982).

Murray, Donald. *A Writer Teaches Writing*, revised second edition, (Boston: Houghton Mifflin, 1985). This is essentially a different book than the first edition with far more information on responding to writing.

Newkirk, Thomas. "Direction and Misdirection in the Peer Response," *College Composition and Communication*, 35 (October, 1984): 300-311.

Sommers, Nancie. "Responding to Student Writing," *College Composition and Communication*, 33 (May, 1982): 148-156.

Stanford, Gene, editor. *How to Handle the Paper Load: Classroom Practices in Teaching English, 1979-1980* (Urbana, Illinois: National Council of Teachers of English, 1979).

# Writing and Literature

# Making Time

by NANCIE ATWELL
*Boothbay Region Elementary School*

"My education was the liberty I had to read indiscriminately and all
the time, with my eyes hanging out."

— Dylan Thomas

**M**Y SISTER CALLED with good news: their offer was
accepted. She, her husband, and my nephew Eric were about
to move to a new house, one with actual closets, a two-car garage, a
big yard with shade trees — and an above-ground pool. Bonnie
called to break the good news, and to warn me. "Please," she asked,
"whatever you do when you visit us, promise you won't let on to
Eric that Atwells don't swim."

My sister wants us Atwells to pretend learning to swim is not a
big deal. Specifically, she wants to be able to dress Eric in life pre-
servers and introduce him to their pool without any adult relatives
betraying our longstanding panic about deep water. Bonnie remembers the swimming lessons of our youth — how our parents conveyed their own unease in the water, how their eyes worried, and
how we kids kept our feet firmly planted touching bottom and
refused to put our faces in the water. We were no fools. We believed
our parents when they showed us that learning to swim was going
to be difficult and dangerous.

My sister knows her smart little boy, like all humans, learns at
least as much from the implicit as the explicit. In defining conditions necessary for learning to take place, Frank Smith refers to
incidents of teaching, implicit and explicit, as "demonstrations."
We humans are surrounded by demonstrations; everything anyone
does "demonstrates not only what can be done and how it can be
done, but what the person doing it feels about the act" (1982, p. 171-
2). We learn by engaging with particular demonstrations, as I
learned more by engaging with my parents' inadvertent demonstrations concerning deep water than from all of their good, explicit
advice about stroking, kicking and breathing.

129

In our classrooms each day, we explicitly teach and students learn; this is a fact, Janet Emig writes, that "no one will deny. But," she continues, "to believe that children learn because teachers teach and only what teachers explicitly teach is to engage in magical thinking ..." (1984, p. 135). It is magical thinking for me to believe I convey to the students in my classroom only my good, explicit advice about writing and reading. The information that comes out of my mouth when I talk is at least equaled by implicit data. Every minute they observe me I'm providing demonstrations with which eighth graders may or may not engage. I can never account for what each learns through the ways I teach.

As the ways my parents approached deep water taught me tacit lessons about swimming, so the ways we approach writing and reading in the secondary English classroom convey inadvertent messages to our students about writing and reading. Recent studies of language arts instruction in U.S. schools, particularly Applebee (1982) and Goodlad (1984), give us a pretty clear picture of exactly how we are approaching writing and reading. We know:

- Our students spend little of their time in U.S. classrooms actually reading: on average, 6% at elementary, 3% at junior high, and, at high school, just 2% of a typical student's school day is devoted to reading.

- Our students spend little of their time in U.S. classrooms actually writing. Only 3% of the writing our students do in school is composing of at least paragraph length.

- Our students spend most of their time in English classes listening to their teachers talk about writing and reading. Between 70 and 90% of English class time is devoted to teacher talk, either lectures or directions.

- When our students are asked to what extent they participate in choosing what they'll do in class, 55% of elementary school kids report having no say; two-thirds of students in grades seven through twelve, students who might reasonably be expected to take on greater individual responsibility, report they do not participate in any way in deciding what they'll do in class.

Teachers mostly decide what students will do in language arts classes. We choose and assign texts, generally one chapter or chunk at a time to be read by the whole class as homework then discussed or formally tested in the following day's session, at the end of which another part of the text is assigned. We present lectures on literary topics and require our students to study and memorize various bits of literary information — characteristics of the New Criticism, the chronology of Shakespeare's plays, lists of Latin roots, literary definitions — followed by exams where students report back what we said and assigned them to memorize. They also complete worksheets and textbook exercises concerned with punctuation, capitalization, sentence structure, paragraph organization, word analysis, and parts of speech. Finally, on occasion their homework consists of a writing exercise where the subject of the writing is an idea of the teacher's.

We talk about the importance of writing clearly and gracefully and reading well and widely, but we seldom make class time for students to write and read, seldom accommodate students' knowledge or choices, and seldom do our students see us writing or reading, see their teachers entering or captivated by the world of written language. Our students are learning from us. The question is, what exactly are they learning? What inadvertant messages do we transmit via this standard approach to the teaching of English? I've begun to try to make explicit both the tacit lessons I learned as a student, as well as those I probably conveyed to my own students for too many years.

### What Schools Demonstrate About Reading and Writing

- Reading and writing are difficult, serious business.
- Reading and writing are performances for an audience of one: the teacher.
- There is one interpretation of a text or topic: the teacher's.
- "Errors" in comprehension or interpretation will not be tolerated.
- Student readers and writers are not smart or trustworthy enough to choose their own texts and topics.

- Intensive, repetitive drill and preparation are necessary before you can read and write independently.

- Reading and writing require memorization and mastery of information, conventions, rules, definitions, and theories.

- Reading and writing somehow involve drawing lines, filling in blanks, circling, and coloring in.

- Readers break whole texts into separate pieces to be read and dissected one fragment at a time. Writers compose whole texts one fragment at a time (punctuation marks, spellings, grammatical constructions, topic sentences, paragraphs, and so on).

- Reading is always followed by a test, and writing mostly serves to test reading (book reports, critical papers, essays, and multiple choice/fill-in-the-blank/short answer exams).

- Reading and writing are solitary activities you perform as a member of a group. Readers and writers in a group may not collaborate, as this is cheating.

- You learn about literature and composition by listening to teachers talk about them.

- Teachers talk a lot about literature and composition, but teachers don't read or write.

- Reading and writing are a waste of the school's time.

- You can fail English yet still succeed at reading and writing.

I know these demonstrations from the inside, as an avid reader and writer who read and wrote only dreaded, assigned texts during my high school years. And I know these demonstrations as a junior high English teacher who spent years teaching the junior high English curriculum, alternately spoonfeeding and forcefeeding one text or assignment after another to my students, dosing them with my English teacher notions of basic skills, appropriate topics for writing, and Great Works of Literature.

Some of this was the same Great Literature I'd been dosed with too, but had eventually come around to loving in college. I was incredulous when I read *Pride and Prejudice* at age twenty, convinced it could not be the same novel I'd suffered through my sophomore year in high school. It took me longer than that to give Willa Cather a second chance. I finally gathered my courage last summer and reread *My Antonia*, eighteen years after barely passing a multiple-choice test on the novel. My list of reconsidered readings goes on and on: *Anna Karenina, The Scarlet Letter, Crime and Punishment, The Mill on the Floss, Hamlet, Moby Dick,* and *The Canterbury Tales* (which I discovered, when I finally got hold of a copy minus the standard high school ellipses, were bawdy).

I was a good reader as a teenager but a different reader — and person — than today. When I was ready for complicated and complex themes and language, those books were there, waiting for me to enter and enjoy. It took me a very long time to consider the implications of my experience as a developing reader for the students who struggled through my courses. My only models for teaching literature were university English education courses that perpetuated litcrit methodologies, and those high school English teachers whose classes I'd endured in my teens. Glenda Bissex observes, "The logic by which we teach is not always the logic by which children learn" (1980). My assumptions about my role as English teacher blinded me to the illogic of my teaching.

Today I teach reading and English, as two separate, daily courses, to all of Boothbay Harbor's eighth graders. A few years ago, on the heels of research showing that sustained silent reading boosted students' reading comprehension, I began letting reading class students choose their own books one period each week, and they began driving me crazy. Daily at least one eighth grader would ask, "Are we having reading today?" We had reading every day — or at least that was my impression. Once again I bypassed an implication for teaching, clinging to each week's four days of curriculum and one day of reading.

My breakthrough in reading finally came by way of writing. Drawing on the work of Donald Murray (1968), Donald Graves (1983), Lucy Calkins (1983) and Mary Ellen Giacobbe, as well as our own classroom research, teachers at my school transformed our daily English classes into writing workshops. I'm going to define a writing workshop as a place where writers have what writers need. Writers need Mary Ellen Giacobbe's three basics of time, ownership, and response (1983).

Writers need regular time set aside *in school* for them to write, time to think, write, confer, write, read, write, change their minds, and write some more. Writers need time they can count on, so even when they aren't writing they're anticipating the time they will be. Writers need time to write well, to see what they think, shape what they know, and get help where and when they need it. Good writers and writing don't take less time; they take more.

Writers need choices. They need to exert ownership, taking responsibility for their writing: their own materials, subjects, audiences, genres, pacing, purposes, number of drafts and kinds of changes to be made, if any. When we invite student writers to choose, they write for all the reasons literate people anywhere engage as writers — to recreate happy times, work through sad times, discover what they know about a subject and learn more, convey and request information, apply for jobs, parody, petition, play, argue, apologize, advise, make money.

Finally, writers need help discovering what they'll choose to do with the time at their disposal. They need response, not at the end when it's too late for our advice to do them any good, but while the words are churning out, in the midst of the messy, tentative act of drafting meaning. In school, this help comes in the form of conferences with the teacher and other students. In writing conferences, students read or describe their writing. Responders begin with information, listening hard to the content of the draft then telling what they hear, asking questions about things they don't understand or want to know more about, and inviting writers to reflect on what they have done and might do next (Graves, 1983).

When I allow time, ownership, and response, I'm expecting students will participate in written language as writers do, that they'll use the writers' workshop to tell their stories. And they do, writing every day for forty-five minutes, an average of twenty finished pieces each year. My whole-group instruction is limited to a mini-lesson of five or ten minutes at the beginning of class on an issue they or I have identified in their writing (Calkins, 1985). Mini-lesson topics include skills issues, such as methods for punctuating dialogue and checking for consistent voice or tense, and process issues: how to brainstorm to find a title, showing rather than telling, deleting and adding information, narrowing the focus of one's content, lead writing.

After the mini-lesson I find out what each writer will do that day, recording my students' plans, and for the remainder of the period writers write, discovering topics, conferring with other writers and with me as I move among them, drafting, revising, and when they've made their best meanings, editing and publishing. All the while I'm offering questions and options. Mary Ellen Giacobbe calls this "nudging" — that gentle guidance designed to move students beyond where they are to where they might be. In all of this, the key is time — regular, sustained time to craft texts, seek help, and plan. Habitual writing makes students writers.

Habitual reading makes students readers. The same qualities that characterize writing workshop have come to characterize my reading course, now a daily reading workshop. I had help here, too, this time from my eighth graders. As they assumed responsibility for their writing, they showed me how their participation in written language could be enriched and extended through reading. The powerful connections they made between their writing and reading dismantled brick by brick the walls I'd erected separating writing and literature. In reading workshop, students have what writers *and readers* need: time, ownership, and response.

Readers need regular time set aside *in school* for them to read, time to think, read, confer, read, reflect, reread, and read some more. Readers need time they can count on, so even when they aren't reading they're anticipating the time they will be. Readers need time to lose track of as they become absolutely caught up in the world of written language. Readers need time to grow.

Readers grow when they exert ownership, assuming responsibility for deciding what and how and why they will read: their own materials, subjects, audiences, genres, pacing, purposes, number of readings and rereadings. When we invite student readers to choose, they read for all the reasons literate people anywhere engage as readers — to live other lives, learn about their own, see how other writers have written, acquire others' knowledge, escape, ponder, travel, laugh, cry.

Finally, readers too need help discovering what they'll choose to do with the time at their disposal. They need response. People who read naturally talk with others as an extension of our lives as readers, sharing opinions, surprises, insights, questions, speculations, and appreciations. Readers don't need lesson plans, study guides, or teachers' manuals. Readers need a text and a listening friend.

Writers and readers need some kind of personal meaning. They need written language to make sense, to give shape to and challenge their worlds. Both writers and readers need to engage naturally and purposefully in the *processes* of written language:

## Writing and Reading as Process

Writers and readers REHEARSE, planning and predicting:

- What will I write?
- What will it be like?
- How will it be shaped by my prior experiences as a writer?

- What will I read?
- What will it be like?
- How will it be shaped by my prior experiences as a reader?

Writers and readers DRAFT, discovering meaning:

- Where will these words I am writing take me?
- Where will these words I am reading take me?
- What surprises, disappointments, problems, questions and insights will I encounter along the way?

Writers and readers REVISE, reseeing and reseeking meaning:

- Is this what I expected, what I hoped for?
- What do I think of those words on the page?
- What new thoughts do I think because of those words on the page?
- What makes sense? What needs to be changed so sense can be made?

Making time for students to read in school invites this engagement. I make time every day for a forty-five minute reading workshop; last year's eighth graders, including eight special education students, read an average of thirty-five full-length works. Reading workshop too begins with a mini-lesson. We spend five or ten minutes talking about an author — Richard Wright, Frost, Lois Duncan, S. E. Hinton — or genre. We read and discuss a poem or a short story by cummings, Updike, Wilbur, London, or one of the kids in the class, peeling away layers of the text and coming to meaning together. We focus on reading and writing processes, how we read and reread the text and how authors might have come to write as they did.

The rest of the period is devoted to independent reading. Students choose their own books, settle back, and dive in. I move along them for the first ten minutes or so, finding out if anyone needs my immediate assistance, and then I sit down and read too, my books and their books. I expect they will read and discover books they love. But I also help, in conferences about their reading.

Most of my talk with eighth graders about literature is written down. We write because writing allows deeper, richer responses than speech, but we write in a special way. For the past two years, eighth graders and I have conferred about literature in letters, thousands of letters back and forth about books, authors, reading, and writing. In our correspondence we nudge each others' thinking. We confirm, challenge, extend, and suggest. And we engage in some serious, and not so serious, literary gossip.

For example, this is an exchange with Jennipher. We're calling each other "Robert" here because one week we happened to read or talk about four works by various authors named Robert; Jenn decided we'd substantially increase our chances of becoming published authors if we were white males named Robert, so she changed our names.

5/2/84

Ms. A. Robert,

Just to see what Anne Frank was going through was miserable. Her "growing up" with the same people everyday. I think she got to know them a lot better than she would have if they weren't in hiding, her mother especially. That sudden change, going into hiding, must have been hard.

It amazed me how much more they went downstairs in the book. [Jennipher had also read the Broadway stage play script of *The Diary of Anne Frank*.] And it seems so much bigger in the book. It also told a lot more of her feelings, right up until the end. It must have come suddenly — to see police come in and arrest them.

I'm going to read some Robert Frost poetry now.

J. J. Robert

P.S.  I think she would have been a writer.

5/3/84

Dear J.J.R.,

I don't have any doubt — if she'd survived, she would have been a writer all her life. Her prose style is so lively, and her insights are so deep. And she loved to write.

We've talked about how movies alter (often for the worst) the books on which they're based. Plays can't help but do the same. All that inner stuff — reflections, dreams, thoughts and feelings — doesn't easily translate into stage action, although Hackett and Goodman tried with Anne's between-act voice-overs.

137

If you're hungry for more information on Anne, please borrow my copy of Ernst Schnabel's *Anne Frank: Portrait in Courage* when Tom Apollonio returns it to me.

Ms. A. Robert

5/10/84

Ms. A. Robert,

We missed you! You get used to peoples' voice. The switch is hard for me.

Robert Frost's poems are really good. "The Witch of Coos" seemed to me somewhere between Stephen King and Ray Bradbury. Kind of wierd, huh? I heard someone quote (kind of!) one of his poems. It was on "People's Court," (Dumb Show) and there was a fight about a fence. In the end the guy came out of the courtroom and was talking to the reporter. He said something like, "This goes to show — good fences don't make good neighbors." I almost freaked out.

Back to the books.

J.J. Robert

5/10/84

Dear J.J.R.,

They quoted Frost on "People's Court"? (You WATCHED "People's Court"?)

I need an aspirin.

N.A.R.

For half of last year, in addition to conferring with me in letters, readers conferred in letters to each other. One day in January, Jane and Arelitsa were passing notes in the back of my classroom. I asked, "What are you two doing?" and Jane said, "Oh, you'll be interested in this." She was right. Their notes were about Frost's "Nothing Gold Can Stay" and what it meant to them, two exuberant thirteen year-olds gossiping about poetry, forging meaning together. So Jane and Arlee put their letters on overheads and shared them with my classes, opening the door to students' exchanges about literature.

Suzy was one of my students that year. She started the year as a lip reader. She used only class time to read and said, "I guess reading is a pretty good thing to do, but sometimes I read and I don't know what I read." By May, Suzy had read nineteen novels. She said, "I really enjoy reading for pleasure. But I hate having books assigned. I can't get into them as much."

Choosing her own books, having time to read and a place to reflect on her reading, Suzy got into books. She wrote the letter below, to her classmate Hilary, at home. It concerns a novel Hilary loaned Suzy, *Mr. and Mrs. Bo Jo Jones*, about a teenage shotgun marriage. In getting into her book, Suzy critiqued the lead and conclusion, connected the novel to her own life, predicted while she was reading what would happen, and made plans to reread.

Hilary,

It's about 12:00 (mignight). I just finished *Mr. and Mrs. Bo Jo Jones*. It was the best book I've ever read in my life.

The book was a slow start and got to be a little boring at times. But the end was fast and different. I loved it! I cried so much. Did you? (I hope so, 'cause I'll feel quite embarrassed about what I'm going to say!)

I didn't cry until right when the doctor and Bo Jo came in to say the baby was dead. It was strange?! I felt so sorry for her (even though it's fiction) for having that happen. Then at the Coffee Pot, when they said it was quits, I was so mad! I knew they were just getting to be very much in love, but thought it probably would be best. I knew for some reason that something good was going to happen when they met at the apartment.

When they sat down and talked and realized they wanted each other but couldn't face it until their decision, it was great. I cryed there too 'cause I was so happy for them! It was great how they went ahead three years and said how it was going. The book was great! I'd recommend it to anyone.

I almost forgot. Did you stop to think if that was you or someone you knew? I did and it seemed so terrible. I thought what if that happened, if I'd do the same. That's not how I wanted to say it, but good enough.

I might want to reread that in the fourth quarter, if you don't mind?

Well, that's all! Finally. I had to right this right now because it was so fresh and I just can't get over how good this book was.

Suzy

P.S. I hope you don't think I'm some sort of freak writing this!!!

Suzy,

Don't worry; you're not a freak!

I'm so glad you liked the book. I know I sure did. I loved all the same parts that you did. I cried too; boy did I.

The book *What About Me?* must be funny. You've been laughing a lot while reading it. What's it about?

Gotta go.

Hilary

Last year, Suzy and her classmates averaged at the seventy-second percentile on standardized reading tests, up from an average at the fifty-fourth percentile when fully 21% scored in the bottom quartile; last year, that figure was just two percent. In June of last year, 92% of my students indicated they regularly read at home for pleasure, and when I asked how many books they owned, the average figure they gave was ninety-eight, up from September's fifty-four. This is the kind of evidence that convinces administrators. I am more convinced by some non-statistical results.

My students discover they love to read. Even the least able, most reluctant readers eventually find the one great book that absolutely impels them, and they are changed readers. For Tim, who never read at home and had never found a book he wanted to reread, the one great book was Jay Bennett's *The Dangling Witness*. Every day for two weeks he came into class waving his copy of the mystery, announcing in an awed voice, "This is a good book. I mean, this is a *really good* book." Until Jay Bennett, Tim hadn't trusted there was such a thing as a good book.

Eighth graders discover authors who write well for them; they learn names of writers whose books they can look for in bookstores and libraries: Frank Bonham, Lois Lowry, Madeleine L'Engle, Cynthia Voight, Anne Tyler, Jack London, Susan Beth Pfeffer, Todd Strasser, Robert Lipsyte, Robert Cormier, Nat Hentoff, Farley Mowat, even, for those ready and willing, Shakespeare. Patrice was ready and willing.

5/17/84

Dear Ms. Atwell,

I finished *Macbeth* today. The reason I decided to read *Macbeth* was because a girl at Skyway Middle School, who I am friends with, read it and really loved it.

I found that the three witches were my favorite characters. Many movies have used take-offs of these characters. *The Beast Master*, a movie I saw on cable, did. They used them differently, but they were used to tell the future.

macbeth himself was, overall, a very confused guy. His wife made him kill the king, and he was hearing voices that told him to "sleep no more." Putting one of Shakespeare's plays into movie form could almost be as bad as Steven King, because of all the killing and walking around with people's heads.

I truly enjoyed *The Comedy of Errors*. I enjoyed the way the two characters called Dromio spoke. Every time they opened their mouths they spoke in riddles. The overall idea was very good and funny. The reunions were like this: 2 father-son, 3 husband-wife, 2 brother, and 2 owner-slave. There is one wedding. Some of the reunions are *very* technical.

Patrice

Eighth graders discover their own theories about literature. Patrice's remark about "technical reunions" has its roots in a discussion that had taken place about a month before. We were talking about Hardy's poem "The Man He Killed" and Mike said, "Ms. Atwell, I really don't like this poem. I mean, why couldn't he just say it in regular language?"

Mike had been reading Frost and Wilbur. He loved e e cummings. He wasn't asking for colloquial prose when he said "regular language."

I said, "Show me what you mean, Mike," and he read the line, "We should have set us down to wet right many a nipperkin" — a word I'd had to look up the night before and could find only in our *O.E.D.*

I'd made a dumb assumption. I thought my kids knew language changed over time, that English wasn't just American and contemporary. So we talked. Over the next weeks kids began collecting and bringing to class examples of prose and poetry from other times. When they hit Shakespeare, I made copies of speeches from five of the plays and we looked at how the language differed within the plays, how Romeo and Juliet spoke one way, Macbeth another, and why. We began to puzzle out what makes a tragedy a tragedy and a comedy a comedy. They decided just about everyone dies in a tragedy and a new order begins; in a comedy, almost everyone gets married, reinstated, or reunited. John said, "Yeah, just like on 'Love Boat.' " And from there we talked about basic plot conventions through all of literature, and how and where Shakespeare had borrowed his plots. Then they found and read to each other stories from Greek and Roman mythology.

They and I were collaborating as theorists, discovering, testing, and acting on literary principles. As readers, eighth graders discovered literature is accessible; that literature is reading, and reading is sensible, interesting, and fun.

As writers, eighth graders discovered they could draw on their experiences as readers, trying out the themes, styles, and modes they read and finding their own voices in collaboration with the voices they love to read. Dede and Billy loved Robert Frost. They collaborated with him by borrowing the theme from "Nothing Gold Can Stay," Frost's poem about the inevitability of change:

### Dawn

The lake sparkled
in the light of the moon.
Dawn was near —
it would be soon.
The clouds gave off a goldish light
and broke the silence of the night.

Now the dawn has come to be noon,
just like grown-up life — all too soon.

Billy Snow

### Beyond the Light

The sunset is so lovely,
with its warm colors and bright glow.
I could sit and stare for hours
at the elegant sight.
Then I shiver
as a cold breeze blows —
to warn me of the darkness
and to warn me of the night.

Dede Reed

Luanne collaborated with John Updike. Her poem arrived at my house in the mails during April vacation, when Luanne was in the middle of basketball tournaments. She borrowed her subject, learning from Updike that basketball was a suitable poetic topic, and she borrowed a simile from his description of the "Ex-Basketball Player" whose hands were "like wild birds":

### The Turnover

I was going for a lay-up
as I remember it;

the brown leathered ball
under my hands,
through half-court
and down toward the middle.

When suddenly the rhythm

stopped.

A hand came down
in place of mine —
like a bird doing
a wild dive:

Just empty space
between my hands
and the floor.

I stood there
wondering where I'd gone wrong,

when I looked up to see
two more points
added to the other side's score.

Luanne Bradley

I've made some discoveries too. I've learned that by giving students more time to learn reading, I've given myself more time to teach reading. I have much less homework than in the old days of lesson plans, lectures, ditto masters, and essay tests. Reading workshop is a workshop for me, too, as I quietly confer with readers, answer letters, and read.

I've learned about adolescent literature, a genre virtually nonexistent twenty years ago when I was an eighth grader. My students introduced me to authors of juvenile fiction who write as well for adolescents as my favorite contemporary novelists — Atwood, Tyler, Heller, Updike — write for me.

I've learned to fill my classroom with books — novels, and also short stories, biographies, histories and poetry, as many paperbacks as I can buy or budget.

I've learned that good, rich discussion of literature happens naturally when real readers are talking together, as opposed to the sterile, grudging responses given by too few students to my old, lesson plan questions. I've learned the context of students' self-selected texts is ripe for high-level literary talk about such traditional teacher's manual issues as theme, genre, and technique. I've learned it's entirely possible to go beyond these to consider reading process, professional authors' processes, relationships between reading and writing, between one text or author and others, between literature and real life.

My students taught me they loved to read. They showed me in-school reading, like in-school writing, could actually do something for them, that the ability to read for pleasure and personal meaning, like writing ability, is not a gift or a talent. It comes with the freedom to choose and with time to exercise that freedom. I learned that freedom to choose and time to read in school are not luxuries. They are not complements to a good literature curriculum. They are the wellspring of student literacy and literary appreciation.

If my class schedule were more typical — that is, forty-five minutes a day for English, including literature — I'd continue to give over class time to reading and writing. But I'd teach writing on three regular, consecutive days, so students would experience that sense of routine and continuity writers need, and follow it with two days of reading workshop, encouraging kids to take home over the weekend those books they read in class on Thursday and Friday. And I would continue to nudge, pointing students toward new topics, modes, styles, authors, techniques, books, and genres.

The most recent National Assessment of Educational Progress reports that American thirteen- and seventeen-year-olds do less reading, especially of fiction, than our nine-year-olds. In a feature in the *New York Times* about Americans' reading habits (Fiske, 1983), Jan Marsten of the University of Chicago suggested that "there seems to be periods in the life-span during which reading tends to drop off, including adolescence. It would hardly be surprising if people did less reading during periods of such upheaval in their lives."

Secondary teachers know about upheaval in adolescents' lives. First jobs, first cars, first boyfriends and girlfriends are hallmarks of adolescence. So are a preoccupation with peers and participation in junior and senior highs' extracurricular activities. Reading necessarily takes a back seat as teenagers' worlds become impossibly full. A former student of mine anticipated April vacation of her freshman year by saying, "Ms. Atwell, I'm going to read six books this week. All of them are books I've been dying to read since Christmas. I just look at them and feel depressed. There's always something else I've got to do." When reading doesn't happen at school, it's unlikely to happen away from school, which means it's unlikely to happen at all.

English teachers can help. We help by giving reading — and writing — our highest priority; we do so when we make time for them to happen in our classrooms. What single, more powerful demonstration can we provide our students of the value we place on these activities? Encircling this are other compelling demonstrations — of the uses of literacy, of writing and reading as whole, sense-making activities, of the ways an adult finds meaning and pleasure in her own and others' written expression, of *all* students' rights as literate human beings.

Genuine, independent reading and writing are not the icing on the cake, the reward we proffer gifted twelfth graders who've survived the curriculum. Reading and writing are the cake. Given what we know about adolescents' lives and priorities, can we afford to continue to sacrifice literate school environments for skills environments? For multiple choice and essay question environments? For spoonfed and forcefed environments? I say we can't. Making time makes readers and writers, and readers and writers can re-make their worlds, using language to see and shape their lives as Jennipher did in her final letter to me.

6/8/84

Dear Ms. A. Robert,

I finished *Autumn Street*. It was excellent how she told it from her childhood view of things, her feelings and then how she was back in the present in the end.

Sunday morning was special. The cats were under my bed at 4:15 doing something, I don't know how they got upstairs. I took them down and looked out the window. Low and behold, sunrise! But no, it did not rise. All I could see was a golden strip across the sky. I pulled up a chair and put my feet up. I said "Nothing Gold Can Stay" in my mind without stumbling and found how Ponyboy could have felt in *The Outsiders*. After fifteen minutes when the sun didn't appear I went back to bed feeling new.

We're really going to miss you.

See you sometime.

J.J. Robert

## References:

Applebee, Arthur. *Writing in the Secondary School: English and the Content Areas.* Urbana, Illinois: National Council of Teachers of English, 1982.

Bissex, Glenda. *GNYS AT WORK: A Child Learns to Write and Read.* Cambridge, Massachusetts: Harvard University Press, 1980.

Calkins, Lucy. *Lessons from a Child.* Portsmouth, New Hampshire: Heinemann, 1983.

_____. *The Art of Teaching Writing.* Portsmouth, New Hampshire: Heinemann, 1985.

Emig, Janet. "Non-Magical Thinking: Presenting Writing Developmentally in Schools." In *The Web of Meaning.* Montclair, New Jersey: Boynton/Cook Publishers, Inc., 1983.

Fiske, Edward B. "Americans in Electronic Era Are Reading as Much as Ever." *The New York Times,* September 8, 1983; p. 1.

Giacobbe, Mary Ellen. Classroom presentation to the Northeastern University Summer Writing Institute, Martha's Vineyard, Massachusetts, July, 1983.

Goodlad, John. *A Place Called School.* New York: McGraw Hill, 1984.

Graves, Donald H. *Writing: Teachers and Children at Work.* Portsmouth, New Hampshire: Heinemann, 1983.

Murray, Donald. *A Writer Teaches Writing: A Practical Method of Teaching Composition.* Boston: Houghton Mifflin, 1968, 1985.

Smith, Frank. *Writing and the Writer.* New York: Holt, Rinehart and Winston, 1982.

# Looking for Trouble: A Way to Unmask Our Readings

by THOMAS NEWKIRK
*University of New Hampshire*

T HE PAST DECADE has seen an attack on the myth of the inspired writer. Linda Flower has traced this myth to Coleridge's account of the creation of "Kubla Khan."[1] According to Coleridge the idea for the poem came without conscious effort; it came fully assembled; it did not require time-consuming choices; and, because it was a gift from the gods, the process of achieving the poem could not be repeated. While Flower does not deny the existence of these Eureka moments, she does argue that this myth breeds passivity on the part of the student who then wants to wait by an open window for inspiration to strike. Fortunately, the testimonies of published writers and the protocols that researchers like Flower have elicited have done much to dispel such myths. Textbooks now go to great lengths to suggest that writing involves a range of choices under conscious control.

Less attention has been given to myths of "inspired reading." Students frequently speak of the "hidden meanings" of poetry, and by that expression they usually mean hidden from them but open to another class of readers — professional readers, teachers. So long as the process of interpretation is unrevealed, myths of inspiration can persist; students will claim that they cannot read poetry because they are not good at getting hidden meanings. The poem comes to be viewed as a Tarot card.

Traditional practices of teaching literature in introductory courses promote the view of "inspired reading" because they obscure the process of forming an interpretation. In the traditional

147

classroom the instructor rarely reveals what happens in his or her initial contact with a poem. I recently asked a group of senior English majors whether they had ever seen a literature professor read something for the first time. None had. Indeed it could be argued that many would have resented a professor assigning a poem he or she had not read, coming to class without having read it, and then winging through it, fumbling as we all fumble on any first encounter. Our evaluation forms tell us that we should come to class prepared. But preparation can be a mask hiding the very process we expect students to master. Our prepared certainty belies the uncertainty of the earlier part of our reading, and by withholding our fumbling from students we can misrepresent the process we claim to teach. If students never see instructors confused, never see them puzzled by a particular usage, never see how an interpretation is revised in subsequent readings, it is logical for the students to conclude that reading is inspired in the same way that Coleridge's composition of "Kubla Khan" was inspired.

There is also little room for uncertainty in the writing required in the traditional introductory course. The mainstay, of course, is the critical analysis paper. Because this type of writing does not exist outside the academic community, its justification presumably is that it helps the student engage with the text. But the constraints of this form seem to preclude the muddling that occurs when readers confront difficult texts for the first time. Most critical analysis papers are supposed to contain a thesis, stated early in the paper; this thesis is subdivided, and each subdivided point must be supported with evidence from the text. The purpose of such writing is to demonstrate a coherent reading, not to explore the possibilities of the incoherencies in a reading. The tone frequently is that of a lawyer, not a reader.

The standard complaint about these papers is that the student fails to probe a response, that the generalizations while supported do not take the student very far into the work. David Bartolomae suggests that the tyranny of the thesis may inhibit inquiry:

> When, for example, we ask students to write about texts, the tyranny of the thesis often invalidates the very act of analysis we

hope to invoke. Hence, in assignment after assignment, we find students asked to reduce a novel, a poem or their own experience into a single sentence, and then to use the act of writing in order to defend or "support" that single sentence. Writing is used to close a subject down rather than to open it up, to put an end to discourse rather than to open up a project?

Like Bartolomae I feel that the traditional critical analysis paper may discourage students from dealing with reactions that are not easily resolved into a thesis, that they may discourage the student from dealing with the more puzzling (and very likely more complex) issues of meaning and language, that, in sum, they encourage the student to play it safe.

In a recent summer school freshman English course I experimented with a different approach to writing about literature that dealt directly with the issue of certainty in reading. Once a week for five weeks the class and the instructor (a graduate assistant) read and wrote about a poem that I selected? I passed around a photocopy of each poem with the name of the poet removed. Both instructor and students then marked words, phrases, lines, whatever gave them difficulty. On each reading they changed their instrument for marking to help indicate the progression of the reading. After the readers had resolved the difficulties (or had worked as hard toward resolving them as they wanted to), they each wrote a narrative account of the reading, using the markings to cue their memory. Once the accounts were written, students and instructor shared the stories of their reading.

This procedure was designed, first of all, to put the instructor and the students on roughly the same footing. All were meeting the poem for the first time; the instructor could not meet the student with a prepared reading. Secondly, the method suggested to the student that the reading of poems involved difficulties and that rereading the poem was one way of working through the difficulties. Finally, the students and the instructor were able to write about difficulties that went unresolved in their readings. As might be expected, many of these unresolved difficulties were evidence of their deepest probes into the poem.

I have grouped the identified difficulties into four very rough categories. The first kind is not so much identifies as exhibited; it involves what Martin Minsky calls dealing in "attitudes." Though writing about the use of the computer, Minsky makes telling comments about any act of thinking:

> [T]hinking is a process, and if your thinking does something you don't want it to you should be able to say something microscopic and analytic about it, and not something enveloping and evaluating about yourself as a learner. The important thing in refining your thought is to try to depersonalize your interior; it may be all right to deal with other people in a vague global way — by having "attitudes" toward them, but it is devastating if this is the way you deal with yourself!

Minsky's term "depersonalize the interior" may at first seem antithetical to the act of reading poetry; clearly the act calls for the engagement of feeling and prior experience. But Minsky correctly identifies the debilitating effect of assigning blame when confronted with difficulty. This blame can either be assigned to the creator of the difficulty, in this project to the willful obscurity of the poet, or more frequently, to the reader himself or herself.

Both types of blame-laying were evident in the student responses. Some took the Poem-as-Tarot-card view and simply confessed inability to deal with such mysteries:

> If there was some hidden meaning [to "Death of a Naturalist": see Appendix] I missed it. Just as most of the poems we have done thus far, the author's hints to the meanings behind the poem slipped me. After I finished the first reading I went back and read it again, but still there was nothing. . . . At the end of most of these poems the depth still leaves me unknowing. I usually look for the title to help. *I guess I just haven't got a great or even good poetic mind.*

Another reader, one who turned out to be perhaps the most perceptive respondent in the class, interspersed her first protocol with admissions of inadequacy:

> Admittedly, I get easily confused and frustrated. Always have and always will hate poetry. . . . My only comment is that I do not like PUZZLES, MYSTERIES, OR POETRY. All are frustrating; none worth the effort.

Other responses shifted the anger to the poet or poem. One student wrote the following concluding statement:

> Bull. While many of the images are nice, the general choppiness should have been smoothed over. Also some of the key words need to be expanded or explained in greater detail.

Whether the blame is placed on the poet or on the reader, the result is the same — the inquiry stops. The students have withheld what Michael Polanyi calls their "personal allegiance"; in order to grant this allegiance the learner must "believe before he can know." The belief is two-fold. There is belief in the learner's own ability, and there is a confidence in others that manifests itself in "anticipation that what he tried to understand is in fact reasonable." Granting allegiance, then, becomes "an act of heuristic conjecture — a passionate pouring of oneself into untried forms of existence" (*Personal Knowledge: Toward a Post-Critical Philosophy* [Chicago: University of Chicago Press, 1958], p. 208).

The other difficulties involve the attempt to "grant allegiance" to the act of reading. As might be expected many of the comments about the initial readings centered on difficult vocabulary, particularly in "Death of a Naturalist" and "The Grace of Geldings in Ripe Pastures."

> In reading this poem through for the first time, I got stuck in a few places — I'm not sure what "bluebottles" means or refers to. And "jampotfuls of jellied specks"? Why would he want them displayed at home? But when I gave up there and read on to the next two lines, I realized he meant a jarful of frogspawn that he was watching hatch into tadpoles. So that section pretty much explained itself.

> For starters, I was reading the words [in "The Grace of Geldings in Ripe Pastures"] wrong. "Timothy" was read as a person's name. I was misreading it in the beginning.

Students generally used one of three strategies for deciphering problem words — looking them up, guessing their meaning from context, or "satisficing," assigning a general plausible meaning to the word and going on.

The instructor frequently shared her struggles with the basic sense of the poems. She (and several students) found the opening line of "Tornado" problematic: "Four farms over it looked like a braid of black hemp." To make sense of the line one must pause as if for a comma before "it." For example, one student wrote: "At the outset I was unsure what was happening because I didn't know what the farms looked on." The teacher had the same difficulty and specified the nature of the problem:

> It was not until the third reading that I finally figured out that the "four farms" *were not* "over it" but rather that the beginning was a naming of location. "It" was confusing up until then — was "it" the tornado — no syntactically that didn't work.

During the class discussion following the exercise almost all of the students agreed that they had precisely the same problem.

A third type of difficulty is one George Steiner calls "contingent difficulties." Here the poem "articulates a stance toward human conditions which we find essentially inaccessible or alien. The tone, the manifest subject of the poem is such that we fail to see a justification for poetic form, that the root occasion of the poem's composition eludes or repels our internalized sense of what poetry should or should not be about" (*On Difficulty and Other Essays* [New York: Oxford University Press, 1978], p. 28). For many students this type of difficulty occurred in reading "The Grace of Geldings in Ripe Pastures." The conclusion of the poem describes the geldings as they "one by one let down / their immense indolent penises / to drench the everlasting grass / with the rich nitrogen / that repeats them." The students balked:

> I found the poem rather interesting. The climax, however, was a disappointment and seemed in bad taste. . . . The last stanza was a let down because I expected something wild, beautiful and splendid, and instead I got a bunch of horses going to the bathroom.

Another student on her copy of the poem circled the last line and wrote, "Disgusting. Visually repugnant. Eating piss-covered grass is what makes them so graceful? Oh Joy!" These responses differ from the first category "dealing in attitudes" in that both readers had worked through the poem, and, at least provisionally, they had given their personal allegiance to the act of reading it. Yet it so violated their sense of the matter for poetry that they were unable to take the role cast for them by the poet.

A fourth and more complex problem had to do with the relationship of images. Many of the instructor's comments were in this category. She commented, for example, on the difficulty with two lines in "Tornado": "and the sky is about to step down / On one leg." She writes:

> [This line] still poses problems for me. I like the feel of it, the way it sounds, the possibility of action but I can't quite see it no matter how hard I try to conjure it up in my mind — I keep trying to have clouds "step down / on one leg."

Sometimes these difficulties were with sets of images. In "Tornado" there are two sets of images that to many of the students had no direct connection: the images of the tornado and the images "of the bulls my father slaughtered every August / How he would pull out of that rank sea / A pair of collapsed lungs, stomach, / Eight bushels of gleaming rope he called intestines." One student worked at reconciling these images as follows:

> The first time through the poem it seemed to make no coherent sense except for the lines of the first stanza reminded me of the tornados I'd seen and lived through in Nebraska. During the second reading I realized that . . . the rest of the poem seemed disjointed from any experience I had ever had with tornados. The third time through was no more enlightening about what the second and third stanzas were trying to put across to the reader. My fourth time through was when it all came to light after just a little thinking and reflection; it dawned on me that he is comparing his father and the slaughter of bulls to the tornado and its devastating properties of retching things right from the ground.

In one response to "Moss Gathering" a student laboriously worked his way through the transitions in the poem that he found difficult, only to encounter a new problem in his third reading. It suddenly occurs to him that there is a conflict between his image of moss gathering and the ominous set of words that the poet uses to describe this activity: "afterwards I always felt mean, . . . / By pulling off flesh from the living planet; / As if I had committed, against the whole scheme of life, a desecration."

> This is really far-fetched, but I get the feeling of impending doom as I read this. "Cemetary," "old-fashioned," "hollow," "underside," "old," "natural order of things," "pulling off the flesh," "desecration," and "went out" all bring to mind scenes of death/destruction. Lord, I don't get it. He's talking about moss-gathering, etc. Why should he be interested in how/why things die? . . . I don't see the connection. All of the transitions are fairly clear now so long as I don't hang up on the "evil" words.
>
> Concluding statement: What the hell is going on?

The writer of this response may feel that after considerable work he still doesn't know what the hell is going on, but his response suggests otherwise. In this and many other responses, the ability to clearly define a reading difficulty suggests considerable insight into the poem.

This specification of difficulty often fits the model of problem-solving developed by John Dewey in *How We Think* (Boston: D. C. Heath, 1933). In this model, problem-solving begins with an interruption of activity. Our ordinary course of action will not work, or two or more competing possibilities confront us, and we must maintain a state of suspense in order to inquire further. In the second stage, which Dewey calls intellectualization, the perplexity of the first stage is pinpointed:

> Our uneasiness, the shock of the disturbed activity, gets started in some degree on the basis of observed conditions, of objects. The width of the ditch, the slipperiness of the bank, not the mere presence of the ditch, is the trouble. The difficulty is getting located and defined; it is becoming a true problem, something intellectual, not just an annoyance. (pp. 108-109)

In the response to "Tornado" quoted above we see this movement. The difficulty begins with a sense of incoherence, in what Dewey calls an "emotional quality" that pervades the experience. On subsequent readings this general sense is given conscious definition; the reader discovers that the root of the sensed incoherence is in the relationship of the first stanza to the rest of the poem. The reader then proceeds to generate a hypothesis to account for the relationship. In the response to "Moss-Gathering" we see a move to intellectualization; the reader notices a sense of "uneasiness" and then goes on to specify the "observed conditions" that can explain his uneasiness.

Thus far I have included excerpts from student and instructor responses to illustrate types of difficulties encountered. As a final example I include a complete response written to "Death of a Naturalist" (see Appendix) which more clearly illustrates the movement that can occur over several readings. This response was written by the student who originally claimed that she was "easily confused" and would "always hate poetry."

> First Reading
> In reading this poem through for the first time, I got stuck in a few places — I'm not sure what "bluebottles" means or refers to. And "jampotfuls of jellied specks"? What jellied specks? Why would he want them displayed at home? But when I gave up there and read on to the next two lines, I realized he meant a jarful of frog-spawn that he was watching hatch into tadpoles. So that section pretty much explained itself.
> The second stanza seemed full of fear — "invading angry frogs," "mud grenades," "obscene threats," "slime kings," "gathered for vengeance." Makes it sound like the author is frightened by these

masses of grown frogs. Sounds like he is afraid these big frogs will punish him for removing frogspawn to take home in the first place; like a big guilt complex.

Don't understand how the title ties into the poem yet — I assume the author is a naturalist, but he's not DEAD . . .

Second Reading

I get the impression the second time through that the author was describing his first year in the location of the poem. "I had not heard before" — but it's a seasonal occurrence — in the reproductive cycle of frogs. But then he did mention "every spring" that he was collecting frogspawn — maybe this was the first time he'd seen the summer phenomena and didn't expect so many frogs (power in numbers he thinks?). I think I understand the title now, though the author describes about learning about frogs in school and watching them hatch — ties them into nature by frogs turning color with the weather. Makes it sound like he was so fascinated by watching them hatch that maybe he was thinking about becoming a naturalist when he grew up or maybe "naturalist" was just his interest in the natural process of frog reproduction. . . .

"Bluebottles" still baffles me — finally looked it up in the dictionary and it's a blowfly that's blue that makes a loud buzzing sound. I've never seen one, but at least that sections makes sense.

The last line of the poem seems very significant; he was so scared and intimidated by the masses of ugly creatures that he was afraid that the frogs might capture and torture him for stealing any more of their "babies." Scared him so much that he apparently decided not to gather frogspawn any more — didn't want anything to do with it he was so scared. The experience rather "killed" his interest in that aspect of nature as a whole or else abolished his possible ideas of becoming a true naturalist — either way it means about the same.

Third Reading

Reading it through for the final time it all goes together and makes perfect sense to me. (Can't believe it — it's too easy — I *must* be missing something.) I looked specifically for major shifts this time. Biggest, most apparent shift is between two stanzas — goes from fascination with frogspawn and frog theory to the horrors of a densely populated area of grown frogs. "Sub-shift" in the first paragraph is between watching tadpoles hatch and learning about frogs in school — practical and theoretical.

I liked this poem because it was pretty easy to figure out and it all made sense to me. Good descriptive writing — I can picture everything the author is saying.

Easy to figure out, perhaps. But the response illustrates a complex and highly effective approach to reading the poem. The function of each reading is distinct: the first works through difficulty with vocabulary and locates a major problem; the second works through the problem; the third consolidates the analyses of the earlier readings and makes them "all go together."

Through these readings the reader circles the fundamental problem posed by the title with its two key terms, "death" and "naturalist." In what sense is the child a naturalist? And in what sense does he die? After all, as she notes at the end of her first reading, "He's not DEAD." In her second reading, she developes two alternative definitions for "naturalist" — either the boy will become a naturalist by profession or he is a naturalist now because of his interest in frog reproduction. With this definition in hand she can test it to see how either or both of these "naturalists" dies and concludes again that the final experience could kill off both; the experience could shake his ambition to become a naturalist, or it could "kill" his interest in frog reproduction. This protocol particularly illustrates the capability of this approach to show how understanding emerges, how a reading is composed.

Once students and instructor had completed the narrative accounts of their readings, these accounts were shared to open the discussion. In each case it became apparent that specific words and images caused problems for almost all the readers, and these common problems became the focus for discussion. For example, much of the discussion of "The Grace of Geldings in Ripe Pastures" focused on the final line — "that repeats them." Both the instructor and many students noted problems with this line in their narrative accounts. When it became clear that this was a common problem, the instructor read from her narrative:

> The meaning eludes me — I can't connect "rich nitrogen" with "repeating" of either the horses or their penises (not sure what "them" in the last line refers to which is connected to not clearly knowing what last line is about).

In her account the instructor specified a difficulty sensed (but sometimes not clearly defined) by many students. The discussion then focused on ways of resolving this difficulty. This procedure led to an openness in the discussion because the working assumption was that all readers experience difficulty. Students were less likely to blame their own problems on an inability to read poetry.

In my initial trial of this procedure the reading accounts were used solely to initiate discussion. Subsequently (with a group of students who were prospective English teachers) I added a further step. After students in the class had written four narrative accounts, I asked them to use these accounts as data and write a profile of themselves as readers of poetry. In James Moffett's terms they were to move from "what happened" to "what happens." This task was more than an exercise in abstraction, though; the assignment pushed students to define themselves as readers and to take inventory of the useful conscious strategies that they employ.

I will quote from the profile of one student:

> I always must size up a poem before I read it, check out its length, its shape. I'm like a general examining the battlefield. Next, read the title, and that always sets up an expectation of what's going to happen. I felt at ease with "Blackberry Picking." It is straightforward, clear. On the other hand, "Mother Ruin" made me cautious and ready for some imagery that might not be clear.

The first reading she describes as a technical reading, usually done out loud, slowly, paying attention to spots that may give her difficulty. If there is a word she doesn't know, she looks it up in her first run through the poem. In the second reading she moves faster, conscious of the problems encountered in the first reading, testing her solutions if she came up with any. Her next reading is a time for savoring the poem:

> At this point, I don't feel finished with the poem. In fact, I haven't experienced it in two readings. This next reading is my favorite. This is where I start to let the poem go. I experience it now by noticing all the marvellous details that give the poem life: "Big dark blobs burned like a plate of eyes," "a rat-grey fungus," and "a glossy purple clot." These are the images that I linger over in these later readings. I appreciate their power. In these later readings (I cannot say final readings because there are no such things) I see the poem as a film with narration. I am the narrator, reading off the script, and, having come to a better understanding of specific problems by looking closely at them, I see the poem. The eye of my mind watches what I read.

In these profiles the text is no longer the poem; rather the writer is "reading" the reading self. The new "text" to be deciphered is the act of reading depicted (imperfectly, of course) in the narrative reading accounts.

In this and almost all the other accounts of readings we can see a mingling of the "subjective" and "objective" responses — to the point that it is difficult to distinguish between the two. Students felt free to express feelings of frustration, confusion, even anger, but these feelings were connected to the text (the extensive marking up of the poem helped here). Similarly, students often referred to personal associations that might help them interpret the poem, but again usually with reference to the poem. Expressions of feeling or personal association rarely floated free of the text. To use Bartolomae's expression, the procedure "opens up" the discourse to allow for the expression of confusion and difficulty in a way that the thesis-controlled critical paper does not. But it also directs the student to specify ways in which the text gives rise to difficulties. It is more text-based than are approaches that direct attention almost exclusively to the reader's feelings and personal associations.

But most importantly, procedures like the one I have described allow us all, teachers and students, to drop the masks that can inhibit learning. We can all act as the fallible, sometimes confused, sometimes puzzled readers that we are. We can reveal ourselves as learners, not always the most graceful of positions. To borrow from the response of one student, we can "show what the hell is going on" with us, and we can ask students to do the same.

## Appendix

### Death of a Naturalist

All year the flax-dam destered in the heart
Of the townland; green and heavy headed
Flax had rotted there, weighted down by huge sods.
Daily it sweltered in the punishing sun.
Bubbles gargled delicately, bluebottles
Wove a strong gauze of sound around the smell.
There were dragon-flies, spotted butterflies,
But best of all was the warm thick slobber
Of frogspawn that grew like clotted water
In the shade of the banks. Here, every spring
I would fill jampotfuls of the jellied
Specks to range on window-sills at home,
On shelves at school, and wait and watch until
The fattening dots burst into nimble-
Swimming tadpoles. Miss Walls would tell us how
The daddy frog was called a bullfrog
And how he croaked and how the mammy frog
Laid hundreds of little eggs and this was
Frogspawn. You could tell the weather by frogs too
For they were yellow in the sun and brown
In rain.

Then one hot day when fields were rank
With cowdung in the grass the angry frogs
Invaded the flax-dam; I ducked through hedges
To a coarse croaking that I had not heard
Before. The air was thick with a bass chorus.
Right down the dam gross-bellied frogs were cocked
On sods; their loose necks pulsed like sails. Some hopped:
The slap and plop were obscene threats. Some sat
Poised like mud grenades, their blunt heads farting.
I sickened, turned, and ran. The great slime kings
Were gathered there for vengeance and I knew
That if I dipped my hand the spawn would clutch it.

Seamus Heaney

## Notes:

1. *Problem-Solving Strategies for Writing* (New York: Harcourt Brace Jovanovich, 1981), pp. 41-43.

3. "Writing Assignments: Where Writing Begins," in Patricia Stock, ed., *FORUM: Essays on Theory and Practice in the Teaching of Writing* (Upper Montclair, N.J.: Boynton/Cook, 1983), p. 311.

3. The poems used were: Robert Hedin, "Tornado," *Poetry*, 140 (1982), 28. Theodore Roethke, "Moss-Gathering," in *Words for the Wind* (Bloomington: Indiana University Press, 1961), p. 43. William Stafford, "Traveling Through the Dark," in *Traveling Through the Dark* (New York: Harper & Row, 1962), p. 11. Seamus Heaney, "Death of a Naturalist," in *Poems 1965-1975* (New York: Farrar, Straus and Giroux, 1980), pp. 5-6. Maxine Kumin, "The Grace of Geldings in Ripe Pastures," in *The Retrieval System* (New York: Viking Press, 1978), p. 67.

4. Quoted in Jeremy Bernstein, "Profiles: Marvin Minsky," *The New Yorker* (December 14, 1981), p. 122.

# Time for Questions: Writing and Literature

*NANCIE ATWELL encourages students to choose their own books. I'm afraid students wouldn't be able to choose well. What can the teacher do to help students choose?*

The teacher, first of all, needs to read and to share her enthusiasm for particular books with students, perhaps through reading aloud excerpts from the book. Just as teachers of writing should be writers, teachers of reading should be readers.

Books also need to be available, and not solely in the school library. Teachers should establish classroom libraries that are bigger than the normal size. In Nancie Atwell's class, for example, there are several hundred books for students. The National Council of Teachers of English published excellent guides for selecting books; see particularly *Your Reading* and *High Interest — Easy Reading*.

There should also be an opportunity for students to share readings, not through formal book reports, but through more casual sharing periods when they may talk briefly about the book, read an interesting passage, and answer questions from other students. This kind of sharing is usually missing in the USSR (Uninterrupted Sustained Silent Reading) periods that are becoming common in many schools. Classrooms can also publish annotated listings of good books where students might write a 3-4 sentence description that might interest someone else in reading the book.

As teachers become familiar with books that appeal to students, they will come up with some "sure winners," books which seem to overpower the most reluctant reader. E.H. Hinton's *The Outsiders* is probably supreme in this category.

*Atwell regularly writes letters back and forth with students. What exactly does she do when she responds to a student's letter?*

She does a number of things. She suggests new books. She talks about reading experiences she has had that are similar to those of the student. She talks about reading habits and processes. But, perhaps most importantly, she helps students view themselves as readers capable of thinking perceptively about books they read. This push toward critical thinking can be seen in a series of letters written early in her course. Her student Tom writes:

> Dear Ms. A.,
>
> I just finished *Jeff White Young Woodsman*. I think it's a good book. It tells about Jeff, born up north then after his parents died at the age of four, moved in with his "so-called" aunt untill he was fifteen. But because he didn't like it their in the city and he didn't like his aunt an uncle he moved up north again with an old friend of his father.
>
> > Tom
>
> P.S.   Is this too "Book Reportish" Is it what you want to hear or read.

> Dear Tom,
>
> As letter stands, it's a little "book reportish," yes. Could you jot me another post script about what made *Jeff White* good?

She is pushing Jeff to define his criteria for good reading and show *why* the book is good. This pushing soon begins to pay off. For later in the month Tom writes:

> Dear Ms. Atwell,
>
> I just finished *Jeff White Young Trapper*. It's the second book in the Jeff White books. If I could cut off the realy mysterious parts I think it would be better. A little mystery is nice but it gets a bit scarry in the hight of it. But other than that it's a good book.
>
> > Tom

Though Tom has not fully explained why the scary parts should be cut, we have the sense that he is a different kind of reader than he was earlier in month. He's not simply someone who gives plot-summary book reports.

*David Bartholomae is quoted as criticizing "the tyranny of the thesis." Isn't there a place for the thesis control paper about literature?*

My view of this question is probably a minority one. I feel that the disadvantages of the thesis-control paper outweigh the advantages — especially for the student who has not had much experience writing about literature. I remember when I had to write these papers, I would pick a thesis that I could support and I would ignore aspects of the poem or story that went counter to my thesis because the purpose of the paper was to *support* that thesis, not to call it into question. Furthermore, the act of channeling my reading into this kind of writing felt most unnatural; my reading bristled with questions, paradoxes, perplexities, but none of this seemed to fit the form I was required to use.

I also feel that literature does not reduce itself easily into single-sentence theses. Think of those embarrassing interviews on TV where the commentator asks someone like Igor Stravinsky — "How would you describe yourself in a sentence?" It's a question that makes a silly assumption — that complex human beings and human behavior is reducible to something only a bit longer than a bumper sticker message. Reading is a continual dialogue with the text, and our generalizations are provisional; like sand castles they don't last for long. My colleague Gary Lindberg has put it well:

> There is something to be said for those truths about texts that supposedly hold their shape independent of the biases of particular readers. They satisfy our wish for something stable, authoritative, and pure. But they are also dead. By their very nature they are irrelevant to the human needs of readers. There is much more to be said for those messier truths that we formulate, undo, and remake again in the human gesture of coming to words. Such truths never last. They are too tentative to connect in elaborate systems of meaning. But they renew our acquaintance with things of the world, they loosen our bondage to a fixed perspective, and they open us to the endless surprise of dialogue with someone else. ("Coming To Words" included in *Only Connect*, Boynton Cook, in press.)

Both the letter writing in Nancie Atwell's article and the reading narratives in my article offer ways to help students work toward, make, and unmake the messier truths Lindberg is talking about.

*Are there other forms of writing that can help students work toward these "messier truths"?*

Students can keep double-entry journals in which students comment on their own understandings of what they read. Ann Berthoff, a major proponent of this type of journal, describes it as follows:

> What makes this notebook different from most, perhaps, is the notion of the double entry: on the right side reading notes, direct quotations, observational notes, fragments, lists, images — verbal and visual — are recorded; on the other (facing) side, notes, summaries, formulations, aphorisms, editorial suggestions, revisions, comment on comment are written. The reason for the double entry format is that it provides a way for the student to conduct that "continuing audit of meaning" that is at the heart of learning to read and write critically. The facing pages are in dialogue with each other. (*The Making of Meaning*, p. 45.)

A student writing on the character Huckleberry Finn might use on side of the journal to make notes about what Huck does and says; on the other side the student could comment on the meaning of these actions — what do they tell us about Huck.

John Dixon suggests a variation of this procedure to encourage students to think about dramatic action. The student selects a section of a play and then keeps a director's notebook on that section. One side of the notebook consists of directions to actors — how will they move, what tones of voice will they use to speak to each other, how will they be positioned on the stage, will their behavior toward each other change in the section. On the other side the student writes a rationale for this action — why do the characters act as they do? (See his essay "What Counts as Response" in *From Seed to Harvest: Looking at Literature* which is available through the NCTE.)

*Should literature be used as models for writing?*

It depends on how the models are used. I don't think professional writing should be used to provide models of "patterns of development" such as compare/contrast, cause-effect, etc. This approach misses the quality that makes the writing good in the first place and instead asks students to view the writing as examples of static patterns. But I do think that literature can provide models of looking at experience; from reading E.B. White we do not get a formal sense of the essay so much as a sense of what it is to view the world like E.B. White.

I like to use short excerpts of literature as models for writing, and one that invariably has an effect is the opening to John Yount's novel, *Trapper's Last Shot*. The novel is set in rural Georgia where, on a sweltering day, five boys go swimming in a river. The first does a cannonball into the water:

> The surface all around, even to the farthest edge, roiled when he hit as if the pool were alive, but they didn't see the snakes at first. The boy's face was white as bleached bone when he came up. "God," he said to them, "don't come in!" And though it was no more than a whisper, they all heard. He seemed to struggle and wallow and make pitifully small headway though he was a strong swimmer. When he got in waist deep water, they could see snakes hanging on him, dozens of them, biting and holding on. He was already staggering and crying in a thin wheezy voice and he brushed and slapped at the snakes trying to knock them off. He got almost to the bank before he fell, and though they wanted to help him, they couldn't help backing away. But he didn't need them then. He tried only a little while to get up before the movement of his arms and legs lost purpose, and he began to shudder and then to stiffen and settle out. One moccasin pinned under his chin, struck his cheek again and again, but they could see he didn't know it, for there was only the unresponsive bounce of flesh.

When students first read this passage, they think that it is the event itself that causes the horror they feel. But I ask them to point to language in the passage that affects them strongly — "face as white as bleached bone," "the unresponsive bounce of flesh" and others. In the discussion students come to see that much of the horror comes from the dispassionate stance of the narrator. In fact, it is *more horrible* because the writer does not use words like "tragic" or "horrible" — the accurate detail creates that feeling of horror in us. I conclude this short discussion by reading some advice from Anton Checkov:

> In the second story, if you have not forgotten, huntsmen wounded an elk. She has the look of a human being and no one has the heart to kill her. Not a bad subject, but dangerous in this respect, that it is hard to avoid sentimentality; the piece has to be written in the style of a police report without words that arouse pity, and should begin like this: "On such and such a date huntsmen wounded a young elk in the Daraganov forest." But should you moisten the language with a tear, you will deprive the subject of its sternness and of everything deserving attention.

I also use literary models to show students how they can expand time — develop fully an incident that may have taken only a few minutes. Time expansion is a new idea for many students who write what I call "and then" narratives where the account of an experience is more an inventory of what happened with nothing highlighted or developed. To introduce the idea of time expansion I read from the climax of George Orwell's essay "Shooting an Elephant."

Although the initial shooting takes only a few seconds it is described in painful detail. After the reading I ask students to think of an experience lasting no more than 3 or 4 minutes that they remember vividly. During the next class I ask them to write about this experience *leaving nothing out*. The writing that comes out of this assignment has an intensity often missing in their other work.

*Should students' papers be used as models?*

This will occur naturally if there is regular sharing in a class. In fact, student papers are often the best models because they seem within reach while professional models may seem beyond their capacity to emulate. I would even argue that the major virtue of sharing writing in small groups is not to offer constructive feedback, but to help all students in the group see various ways of approaching various topics.

# Suggestions for Further Reading:
## Writing and Literature

Atwell, Nancie. "Writing and Reading from the Inside Out," in Jane Hansen, Thomas Newkirk, and Donald Graves, editors, *Breaking Ground: Relating Reading and Writing in the Elementary School* (Portsmouth, N.H.: Heinemann Educational Books, 1985).

Berthoff, Ann. *The Making of Meaning: metaphors, models, and maxims for writing teachers* (Montclair, N.J.: Boynton/Cook, 1981).

Bleich, David. *Readings and Feelings: An Introduction to Subjective Criticism* (Urbana, Illinois: National Council of Teachers of English, 1975).

Fillion, Bryant. "Reading as Inquiry: An Approach to Literature Learning," *English Journal*, 70 (January, 1981): 39-45.

Fish, Stanley. *Is There a Text in This Class?: The Authority of Interpretive Communities* (Cambridge, Massachusetts: Harvard University Press, 1980).

Moran, Charles. "Teaching Writing/Teaching Literature," *College Composition and Communication*, 32 (February, 1981): 21-29.

Newkirk, Thomas, editor. *Only Connect: Uniting Reading and Writing* (Deansboro, N.Y.: Boynton/Cook, in press).

Petrosky, Anthony. "From Story to Essay: Reading and Writing," *College Composition and Communication*, 33 (February, 1982): 19-36.

Richards, I.A. *Practical Criticism: A Study of Literary Judgement* (New York: Harcourt, Brace and Company, 1929).

Rosenblatt, Louise. *The Reader, the Text, and the Poem* (Carbondale: Southern Illinois University Press, 1978).

Smith, Frank. "Reading like a Writer" in Julie Jensen, editor *Composing and Comprehending* (Urbana, Illinois: National Council of Teachers of English, 1983).

Tompkins, Jane, editor. *Reader-Response Criticism: From Formalism to Post Structuralism* (Baltimore: Johns Hopkins Press, 1980).

# Writing Across the Curriculum

# Language Across the Curriculum
## Examining the place of language in our schools

by BRYANT FILLION
*Fordham University*

"LANGUAGE ACROSS THE curriculum" and "school language policies" have become familiar phrases among Ontario educators, at least since the publication of the 1977 Ministry of Education guidelines for English at the Intermediate and Senior levels. Following the lead of the 1975 Bullock Report, *A Language for Life*,[1] both Ontario guidelines refer to language across the curriculum, with the Intermediate Guideline stipulating that the school principal "recognizes the role that language plays in all areas of the curriculum and provides the initiative for a school language policy."[2] The Senior Guideline notes that "In all subject areas, the use of language involves the student in the formation of concepts, the exploration of symbols, the solving of problems, the organization of information, and interaction with his or her environment. Teachers need to recognize and reinforce the central role of language in this learning process."[3] A forthcoming Intermediate Guideline supplement, titled *Language Across the Curriculum*, will provide additional information to teachers and administrators trying to find out just what "language across the curriculum" means, and what they are expected to do about it.

While providing considerable impetus for schools to improve their work with students' language, such official mandates can lead to problems as well. Undoubtedly, more than a few English department heads have been caught off guard by a principal's request to

171

"get a school language policy to me by next week." And Gerald Haigh's *Times Educational Supplement* parody of the situation must ring true for many Ontario schools:

> *Monday.* Arriving at school in a decisive mood, I wrote on my 'Things to do' pad:
>
> 1. See the caretaker again about that funny sticky stuff behind the radiator in room three.
> 2. Remove the outdated notices from the board in the corridor.
> 3. Institute a language policy across the curriculum.[4]

### A School's Language Policy

The theoretical basis of language across the curriculum derives largely from the Bullock Report, and the work of people like James Britton,[5] Nancy Martin,[6] and Douglas Barnes.[7] Three central tenets of the concept are that (1) language is more than surface structure, (2) the entire school as an environment influences students' language development, and (3) language plays a key role in virtually all school learning. Based on these assumptions, a school language policy is concerned with more than the elimination of errors in spelling, punctuation, sentence structure, and usage conventions. It involves broadening teachers' notions and awareness of language, helping students learn to use language, and helping them use language to learn. As one publication succinctly states:

> One of the major functions of language . . . is its use for learning: for trying to put new ideas into words, for testing out one's thinking on other people, for fitting together new ideas with old ones, and so on, which all need to be done to bring about new understanding. These functions suggest active uses of language by the pupil as opposed to passive reception. A 'language policy' is more accurately described, therefore, as a 'language and learning policy'.[8]

Language across the curriculum, interpreted as a concern for improving surface structure, usually results in a somewhat grudging agreement from non-English teachers to pay more attention to spelling and sentence structure in their students' papers. The "policy" which results deals largely with the evaluation and marking of student papers.

Interpreted in the broader sense of "language *and learning*," language policies become considerably more radical, raising fundamental questions about learning and teaching. For example, a 1971 discussion document from the London Association for the Teaching of English includes a sample "Language Policy" containing the following items:

> We need to find ways of helping pupils without putting words in their mouths. We could perhaps be less concerned to elicit from them verbatim repetitions of time-honoured formulations than to ensure that pupils engage in a struggle to formulate for themselves their present understanding. Discussion is an essential part of that process. . . .
>
> Many school activities should be carried out by small groups which can use their talk to move towards understanding by means which are not present in the normal teacher-directed classroom. . . .
>
> Written work asks for the teacher's attention and interest more than (perhaps, instead of) his marks. If prior and exclusive attention is given to spelling, punctuation and correctness (in its narrowest sense) then all too easily the writer feels that the message itself and his efforts to communicate it are of less importance.[9]

Even though these statements, and the entire L.A.T.E. document, are intended as tentative guides for discussion, such a policy obviously goes far beyond an agreement to mark spelling and sentence errors in students' papers. And it poses some very difficult problems for implementation, especially in the secondary school, as Nancy Martin indicates:

> . . . the general pattern of the organisation of secondary schools works against it. . . . Apart from pressures of time there are implicit assumptions that a specialist will be able to manage his own affairs — including of course, the language proper to his subject. . . . This problem is compounded by the fact that most secondary teachers (other than some teachers of English) think of language as something to be corrected and improved.[10]

### Existing (Implicit) Policies and "Rules"

Faced with these difficulties, a secondary school staff might well decide to do without a language policy. However, the question is not really whether or not to have a language policy, but whether or not to make the policy explicit. Through the attitudes and actions of individual teachers, the shared assumptions of departments, and the demands and constraints placed on students' language use, every school already has a policy toward language and learning, even though the policy and its effects have probably never been articulated or discussed. For example, the policy in some classes, if not in entire schools, might be something like the following:

> Students will learn by listening and reading, rather than by speaking or writing.
>
> Students will be quiet, unless given permission to speak by and to the teacher.
>
> Students will ask very few questions about the subject.
>
> Students will write down only the words and ideas given to them by the teacher or the textbook.
>
> Students will only speak or write in correct, final-draft language, to demonstrate that they have learned the information given.

This is a parody, of course. But it may be closer to the truth than we suppose. Arno A. Bellack and others, summarizing extensive research into classroom language, indicate that there are several unstated but powerful "rules" which seem to control "the classroom game" for most teachers and students. Among the rules for the pupils are the following:

> The pupil's primary task in the game is to respond to the teacher's solicitations.
>
> In general, the pupil will keep his solicitations to a minimum.
>
> Even more important than the *don't* solicit rule is the *don't* react evaluatively rule. Under no condition is the pupil permitted to react evaluatively to a statement made by the teacher; that is, the pupil does not tell the teacher he is right or wrong, that he is doing well or doing badly.
>
> A corollary of the "don't react evaluatively" rule is the general principle, "within the classroom, teachers speak The Truth."[11]

To the extent that Bellack's findings characterize classroom practice, these rules of the game constitute a language policy very much at odds with current theory and research. Among other things, they quite explicitly deny a key principle of the Bullock Report, that "language has a heuristic function; that is to say a child can learn by talking and writing as certainly as he can by listening and reading."[12] A language policy which severely restricts pupils' language use in the classroom impedes both language development and learning for a great many students. One major function of a school language policy is to bring such limitations to teachers' conscious awareness for examination and possible change.

In my work with school principals, I have tried to indicate the primary concerns of a school language policy from the point of view of a concerned and informed parent seeking a linguistically adequate school for my daughters. The following questions suggest the kind of information I think schools should be seeking about their own language policies and practices:

**Some Questions for the Principal** (From a Troublesome Parent)

In what ways do you want students' language to be different as a result of time spent in this school?

What evidence do you have that students can speak, write, or read better when they leave the school than when they entered?

How much writing do students do in this school? What kinds of writing, and in which subjects?

How many teachers in this school take class time to teach students how to do the kind of writing they require? How many provide opportunity for students to "practise" writing (i.e., without being marked)? How many provide students with models of "good" writing in their subjects?

How many teachers encourage students' "exploratory talk," to put new ideas and information into students' own language?

In an average day (or week) in this school, how much opportunity will an average student have to question, talk, or write about the things she or he is expected to learn? How much opportunity does she or he have to *use* and *apply* knowledge (except on tests)?

How readable and interesting are the textbooks? What additional material is available for students to read about the subjects?

How many students in this school read (or write) for pleasure? What do they read? How many read newspapers regularly? How many are non-readers?

Perhaps it goes without saying that such questions make many principals feel somewhat uncomfortable. But most principals agree that the questions are reasonable, and perhaps even worth the time and energy to find some answers.

### Examining Present "Policies" On Writing

During the 1977-78 school year, I was involved with several schools attempting to establish language policies, especially with regard to writing. In each case, we began by asking questions about present practices, and in three Toronto-area schools we conducted "writing surveys" to obtain answers to three questions: How much writing are students actually doing? What kinds of writing are they doing? In which subjects? The results of the surveys have been illuminating, both to the schools involved and to others as well. They indicate, I believe, both the need for and potential of language policies which involve teachers in gathering data and reflecting on their own practices.

In each of the three schools, the survey was conducted for a two-week period (ten school days), during which time we xeroxed daily all of the writing done in and for school by a sample of students. Insofar as possible, we copied every bit of writing these students did: notes, tests, homework, worksheets, rough drafts, and papers.

The three categories devised to describe the kinds of writing found in the first survey also proved adequate for the two later surveys: *copying* (where the student was simply "taking down" information directly from some source), *directed writing* (where students were writing out answers to teacher or textbook questions primarily dealing with the recall of information, summarizing, or making notes in their own language), and *undirected writing* (involving some degree of original thought or creativity, as in stories or reports on students' own topics, where the writer was involved in manipulating information, ideas, and language. "Open ended questions" involving students in the interpretation and manipulation of content would also presumably result in undirected writing.).

The first survey was conducted in a senior public school (grades 7 and 8) in a middle-class area of Toronto.

---

**SCHOOL A** (Grades 7 and 8)

n = 21 (random sample)

**Amount of Writing in 10 School Days** (average pages* per student)
Grade 7      9.3 pages
Grade 8      9.4 pages

*Note: In tabulating these data, we counted as a "page" any piece of paper with some student writing on it, often just a few words. Therefore, on the basis of this sample, students in this school write considerably less than a page a day.

**Kinds of Writing:** *Copying:* 46 pages (21% of total); *Directed Writing:* 96 pages (43% of total); *Undirected Writing:* 81 pages (36% of total).*

*Note: The sample of writing included very few rough drafts, no examples of informal or "personal" writing, and no examples of extended writing going on for more than two pages.

**Writing by Subjects:** *English and math* (taught together in this school): 90 pages (40% of total); *science:* 66 pages (30% of total); *history and geography:* 56 pages (25% of total); *others:* 11 pages (5% of total).

Perhaps the only additional comment necessary here is that the teachers in this school were quite surprised at how little writing was being done, and at the dearth of writing in the *undirected* category. Subsequent informal observation indicated that both the total amount of writing and the proportion of undirected writing increased in the school following discussion of the survey results by the teachers.

### The Second Survey

The second survey was conducted in a junior high school (grades 7, 8, and 9) in a middle class neighborhood. In an attempt to simplify data collection, the survey was conducted using a small number of "able, cooperative" students, reasoning that this would produce "best case" findings. Presumably other students in the school would be writing less than these good students were. To provide more precise findings, words were counted rather than pages. On the average, students write about 275 words per page of lined notebook paper.

**SCHOOL B** (Grades 7, 8, 9)

n = 11 ("Good" Students)

**Amount of Writing per Week** (average number of words per student per week)

|  | words in continuous, related sentences | isolated words, sentences, phrases | total words per week |
|---|---|---|---|
| Grade 7 (n = 4) | 223 | 117 | 340 |
| Grade 8 (n = 4) | 616 | 210 | 826 |
| Grade 9 (n = 3) | 580 | 760 | 1340 |

**Kinds of Writing** (average words per student per week; % of total for grade)*

|  | copied | directed | undirected |
|---|---|---|---|
| Grade 7 | 92 (30%) | 32 (10%) | 190 (60%) |
| Grade 8 | 187 (23%) | 590 (71%) | 47 ( 6%) |
| Grade 9 | 741 (55%) | 595 (45%) | 0 |

*Note: The sample contained very few rough drafts and no cases of students writing about or reflecting on their own experiences or commenting informally on the subject matter. Directed writing here consisted almost entirely of summarized or paraphrased information. Undirected writing was primarily play scripts and stories for English. In computing these averages, occasional isolated words which had been included in the "amount" tally were disregarded.

**Writing by Subjects** (total words by all students in two weeks; c = copied, d = directed, u = undirected)

|  | English | History Geography | Science | Others |
|---|---|---|---|---|
| Grade 7 | u: 1520 | c: 100<br>d: 260 | c: 76 | c: 564 |
| Grade 8 | c: 50<br>d: 2420<br>u: 350 | c: 660<br>d: 2195<br>u: 25 | c: 639<br>d: 49 | c: 145<br>d: 50 |
| Grade 9 | d: 1693 | c: 4445 | d: 200 | c: 1680 |

Because of the small number of students, and the sampling procedure used, we cannot generalize from this sample to the school population as a whole. Nevertheless, as in the first school, teachers were quite surprised at the limited amount of writing done by these "able" students, and the small proportion of it which could be identified as undirected writing. Following the survey, teachers reportedly worked to increase the amount of undirected writing done in various subjects.

### The Third Survey

The third survey was conducted in a secondary school (grades 9 to 13), using a random sample of 36 students (approximately 2.25% of the student population). Given the random sampling, and the fact that the school is on a semestered system, not all subjects were covered for all grade levels. However, with the exception of art (2 students), family studies (3 students), and geography (8 students), all subjects were represented by at least ten students at various grade levels.

To the extent that School C's findings accurately reflect actual practices, they do indicate a clear "language and learning policy" with regard to writing. Writing is done primarily to improve and demonstrate the retention of information. Writers seldom deal with their own ideas, language, or understanding of material to demonstrate some degree of independent thought and work with the content, and they virtually never write imaginatively, or about their own experiences.

Perhaps predictably, when teachers in this school saw the survey results, their initial concern was that the "quality" of writing had not been reported. They were much more in favor of a policy which would "correct" writing than one which would deal with its uses for learning.

## Learning to Use Language

The primary interest in "language across the curriculum" and "school language policies" has come from a concern with improving students' language, rather than from a concern with language and learning. However, the popular concern with young people's language development has had a narrow focus which invites a correspondingly limited response from schools. So long as the concern with language is limited to such surface specifics as spelling and grammatical correctness, attention is focused on direct instruction and teacher correction, rather than on the larger problems of language functions, intentions, and use.

Linguist Courtney Cazden argues, "The most serious problem facing the language arts curriculum today is an imbalance between means and ends — an imbalance between too much attention to drill on the component skills of language and literacy and too little attention to their significant use." The same pressures which have given needed attention to the importance of language development have done so in such a way as to impede the very progress desired:

> Responding to real or imagined community pressures, able and conscientious teachers all over the country are providing abundant practice in discrete basic skills; while classrooms where children are integrating those skills in the service of exciting speaking, listening, reading, and writing activities are becoming rare exceptions.[13]

Ultimately, of course, such exclusive emphasis on discrete skills will be self-defeating, though it does answer the immediate demand for action in a relatively painless and socially acceptable way. It is certainly far easier to teach (once again) a lesson on run-on sentences and fragments than to follow the advice of the Bullock Report:

> The kind of approach which we believe will produce the language development we regard as essential . . . involves creating situations in which, to satisfy his own purposes, a child encounters the need to use more elaborate forms and is thus motivated to extend the complexity of language to him.[14]

Once we accept as a basic premise that intention and use are essential elements in the development of language, there are important implications for a school as a language environment which promotes or inhibits development. In addition to asking "What are students being taught about language?" we must ask "What opportunities do they have to use language in meaningful ways for a variety of purposes?" The results of our school writing surveys suggest that these opportunities may be very limited indeed. There were very few instances where a student clearly encountered "the need to use more elaborate forms" and virtually none where a student wrote "to satisfy his own purposes."

---

### SCHOOL C (Grades 9-13)

n = 36 (random sample)

**Amount of Writing**

In two weeks, these students wrote a total of 98,890 words, an average of 2746 words/student, or slightly more than one page per day. However, amounts varied widely among students, teachers, and subjects. Most students wrote considerably less than a page a day.

**Amount by Subject** (average words per student per 10 days; average pages per day @ 275 words per page)

|                     | English | History | Geography | Science | Technical | Business |
|---------------------|---------|---------|-----------|---------|-----------|----------|
| avg. wds/-10 days:  | 1323    | 1962    | 1640      | 1360    | 687       | 650      |
| avg. pages/-day:    | ½ +     | ¾       | ⅔         | ½       | ¼         | ¼        |

**Kinds of Writing** (Note: In this survey, the "undirected" category was subdivided into subject-related, personal, and imaginative.)

In the total sample, 37% of the writing was *copied;*
43% was *directed;**
19% was *subject-related undirected;**
1% was *personal undirected*, and
0.05% was *imaginative undirected.*

*Note: Three long grade-13 papers in English and history account for more than half (55%) of all the *subject-related undirected writing*. Most *directed writing* involved answers to factual, recall questions, or longer "reports" which were largely paraphrased versions of encyclopedia or textbook information.

**Kinds of Writing by Subjects** (percents of total writing done in the subject)

|  | copied | directed | subject-undirected | personal undirected | imaginative undirected |
|---|---|---|---|---|---|
| English | 14% | 37% | 47% | 2% | 0.08% |
| History | 47% | 39% | 14% |  |  |
| Geography | 18% | 77% | 4% |  |  |
| Science | 50% | 46% | 4% |  |  |
| Technical | 76% | 24% |  |  |  |
| Business | 35% | 41% | 24% |  |  |
| Family Studies | 38% | 38% | 6% | 18% |  |
| Math | 71% | 25% | 4% |  |  |
| Art |  | 26% | 57% |  | 17% |

As Joan Tough's research indicates, children arrive at school from homes which have provided markedly different opportunities for language use.[15] The Bullock Report notes the implications of these findings for schools:

> If a child does not encounter situations in which he has to explore, recall, predict, plan, explain, and analyse, he cannot be expected to bring to school a ready made facility for such uses. But that is not the same thing as saying the ability is beyond him. What is needed is to create the contexts and conditions in which the ability can develop.[16]

When we concern ourselves with students' opportunities to use language in purposeful ways, rather than in dummy-run exercises divorced from context, we can raise some very powerful and practical questions about school practices. In my work with teachers, I have encouraged them to consider questions such as the following:

How much opportunity do your students have to use their own language to discuss and make sense of your subject; to talk and write to a sympathetic, encouraging audience, interested as much in what they have to say as in correcting what they say; to use language for such logical operations as explaining, describing, defining, giving options, inferring, speculating, comparing and contrasting, questioning, and paraphrasing?

In an average week in your classroom, how often do you *use* an idea or comment volunteered by a student? How often do you encourage a student to elaborate on what he or she has said? How often do you, or your students, ask questions you are genuinely interested in? How many students speak or ask questions voluntarily about the subject? How much voluntary reading do students do? How frequently and how much do students write? How often do they discuss and question what they have read or written?

There is nothing subject-specific to English or language arts in such questions, and in fact teachers of science, geography, family studies, and other subjects seem to find them useful ways to approach the topic of language development in their own subjects. Once teachers see that language use is as important to development as direct instruction and correction, their own role in students' language development becomes much clearer. We must begin, I think, by encouraging teachers of all subjects to look at what they and their students are doing with language, and at the relationship of these language uses both to learning and to language development.

### Using Language to Learn

One major obstacle to the serious consideration of language in schools is that language is so obvious and all-pervasive that it often escapes our attention. Until teachers examine carefully the relationships of language to learning, understanding, and intellectual development, they are unlikely to take seriously their own responsibilities toward language development or to realize the potential of language for all learning. The Bullock Report says, "For language to play its full role as a means of learning, the teacher must create in the classroom an environment which encourages a wide range of language uses."[17] But this principle was clearly not operating in the writing collected in our surveys.

Two key points teachers need to understand about language and learning are that language plays a key role in understanding new information, and language plays a key role in intellectual development. This first point is nicely summed up in the NATE document on language across the curriculum:

> ... theory and practice suggest that if a learner at any level is able to make his own formulations of what he is learning, this is more valuable to him than taking over someone else's pre-formulated language. In practice, this means that pupils often need to have the opportunity to say or write things in their own ways, in their own styles, rather than copying from books or taking notes from dictation.[18]

Douglas Barnes,[19] among others, offers theoretical and research evidence to support the idea that by putting ideas into our own language we come to understand them. When students are denied the opportunity to use language in this way, learning suffers.

Perhaps more important than the immediate role of language in making sense of new information is the part it plays in developing mental operations and intelligence. A decade ago, James Moffett pointed out the relationship in *Teaching the Universe of Discourse:*

> ... a pedagogy based on provoking or eliciting thought presupposes that a child is already capable of generating the required kinds of thoughts. Asking "stimulating" questions and assigning "stimulating" reading invites the student to put out but does not give him anything, as teachers of the disadvantaged know well. In order to generate some kinds of thoughts, a student must have *previously* internalized some discursive operations that will enable him to activate his native abstracting apparatus. ...
>
> Elicitation has a place certainly at some stage of instruction, but more basic is to create the kinds of social discourse that when internalized become the kinds of cognitive instruments called for by later tasks.[20]

Although the exact relationship of thought and language remains a largely uncharted area, there is little doubt that restricted language development is associated with restricted mental operations of the type most called upon by schools. At the very least, language must be accepted as our point of access to students' thinking. Despite many controversies, there are two key points of general agreement, cited in the Bullock Report:

> (a) that higher processes of thinking are normally achieved by the a child's language behaviour with his other mental and perceptual powers; and
>
> (b) that language behaviour represents the aspects of his thought processes most accessible to outside influences, including that of the teacher.[21]

In James Britton's telling phrase, language is "the exposed edge of thought."

It is obviously possible to by-pass a good deal of students' language use in our teaching, by extensive use of teacher lectures and audio-visual presentations, short-answer recitation sessions, workbook "fill in the blank" exercises, "copy from the board" note-taking, and objective tests. Unfortunately, such teaching deprives students of two major means of learning — talking and writing — and it may result in limited intellectual growth as well. As Donald Graves points out in his study of the diminishing use of writing in schools:

> A far greater premium is placed on students' ability to read and listen than on their ability to speak and write. In fact, writing is seldom encouraged and sometimes not permitted, from grade one through the university. Yet when students cannot write, they are robbed not only of a valuable tool for expression but of an important means of developing thinking and reading skills as well.[22]

The language across the curriculum movement has great potential for improving both language and learning, by leading us to examine and reflect on the place of language in our schools in light of such admonitions. If they are not trivialized to an exclusive concern for surface correctness, school language policies may yet provide a salutary outcome to the "back to basics" controversy.

## Notes:

1. Committee of Inquiry appointed by the Secretary of State for Education and Science, Sir Alan Bullock, chairman, *A Language for Life* (London: HMSO, 1975). One of the key recommendations of the report is that "Each school should have an organised policy for language across the curriculum, establishing every teacher's involvement in language and reading development throughout the years of schooling" (p. 514).

2. Ontario Ministry of Education, *Curriculum Guideline for the Intermediate Division English* (Toronto: Ministry of Education, 1977), p. 6.

3. Ontario Ministry of Education, *Curriculum Guideline for the Senior Division English* (Toronto: Ministry of Education, 1977), p. 5.

4. *Times Educational Supplement*, 26.3.76, quoted by Nancy Martin, "Initiating and Implementing a Policy," in Michael Marland, et al., *Language Across the Curriculum* (London: Heinemann Educational Books, 1977), p. 231.

5. James Britton, *Language and Learning* (Harmondsworth: Penguin Books, 1970).

6. Nancy Martin et al., *Writing and Learning across the Curriculum, 11-16* (London: Ward Lock Educational, 1976).

7. Douglas Barnes, *From Communication to Curriculum* (Harmondsworth: Penguin Books, 1976).

8. National Association for the Teaching of English, *Language across the Curriculum: Guidelines for Schools* (London: Ward Lock Educational, 1976), p. 7.

9. In Douglas Barnes, James Britton, and Harold Rosen, *Language, the Learner and the School* (Harmondsworth: Penguin Education, 1971), pp. 163 and 165.

10. Nancy Martin, "Language across the Curriculum: A Paradox and Its Potential for Change," *Educational Review*, Vol. 28, No. 3 (June 1976), pp. 206-219.

11. Arno A. Bellack, et al., "The Classroom Game," in Ronald T. Hyman, ed., *Teaching: Vantage Points for Study*, Second Edition (Philadelphia: J. P. Lippincott, 1974), p. 351.

12. Bullock Report, *op cit*, p. 50.

13. Courtney Cazden, "Language, Literacy, and Literature: Putting It All Together," *National Elementary Principal* (October 1977), pp. 40-41.

14. Bullock Report, *op cit*, p. 67.

15. For a summary introduction to Joan Tough's work, see Robert E. Shafer, "The Work of Joan Tough: A Case Study in Applied Linguistics," *Language Arts* 55 (March 1978), pp. 308-314 +.

16. Bullock Report, *op cit*, p. 54.

17. Bullock Report, *op cit*, p. 188.

18. N.A.T.E., *op cit*, p. 8.

19. *From Communication to Curriculum* (Penguin, 1976). See also Douglas Barnes and Frankie Todd, *Communication and Learning in Small Groups* (London: Routledge & Kegan Paul, 1977), and Douglas Barnes, "Language in the Secondary Classroom," in *Language, the Learner and the School* (Penguin, 1971), pp. 11-77.

20. James Moffett, *Teaching the Universe of Discourse* (Boston: Houghton Mifflin, 1968), p. 70.

21. Bullock Report, *op cit*, p. 49.

22. Donald H. Graves, "Balance the Basics: Let Them Write," *Learning* (April 1978), p. 30.

# Journals across the Disciplines

by TOBY FULWILER
*University of Vermont*

*When I write a paper I make it personal. I put myself into it and I write well. It bothers me when people tell me to make it more personal — to take me out of it, I'm afraid I can't write unless I am in the paper somehow.* (Jody S.)

STUDENT WRITING will not improve by simply increasing the number of writing assignments in a course, adding a term paper, or switching to essay tests. While these changes may be appropriate for some disciplines, they are not for others; in any case, such changes alone will not significantly alter the quality of student writing. Students do need to write often, and in every discipline, but equally important is the *kind* of writing students are asked to do.

Research by James Britton and his colleagues at the University of London suggests that the writing taught in schools today is narrowly conceived. Britton describes writing according to three "function categories": "transactional," language to get things done — to inform, instruct and persuade; "poetic," language as an art medium — poetry and fiction; and "expressive," language written for oneself — thinking and speculating on paper.[1] In looking at two thousand pieces of writing from sixty-five secondary schools, Britton found that 84% of the writing by high school seniors was transactional. Poetic writing accounted for less than 7% of school writing, and expressive less than 4%[2]

Few teachers ask their students to write in the expressive mode, which may suggest that few teachers value this form of writing. Britton believes this must change, insisting that expressive writing is both the matrix from which other forms of writing take shape and the language closest to thought. Expressive writing "may be at any stage the kind of writing best adapted to exploration and discovery. It is the language that externalizes our first stages in tackling a problem or coming to grips with an experience."[3] Expressive writing characteristically is unstructured; it finds shape most often in letters, first drafts, diaries, and journals.

Janet Emig's research in the United States parallels Britton's work in England.[4] Emig points out that first-utterance, expressive writing, which she calls "reflexive," is essentially a form of thinking, "a unique mode of learning," different from talking, reading, and listening.[5] As an aid to learning, the writing "process" is even more important than the written product. The "process" of writing exercises and influences the process of thinking, while the product of writing — the term paper, lab report and essay exam — evaluates and measures student performance. Britton and Emig agree that some forms of student writing need to be evaluated; however, they also suggest that the current school practice of stressing only the transactional product-oriented writing has a negative effect on the writing and learning abilities of students.

One writing activity which focuses both student and teacher on the learning process of writing is the student journal. In *Hooked on Books* (1966), Dan Fader urged all high school teachers to use journals in their classrooms: "I have seen journals in public schools used for continuing book reports in English classes, for observations upon municipal government in civics classes, and as diaries in social studies classes."[6] Journals offer a variety of writing activities to college students in all disciplines. Field notes jotted in a biology notebook and sifted through the intellect can become an extended observation written in a "biology journal"; this entry, in turn, might become the basis for a major project. Personal responses by history students in their journals may increase the understanding of distant and confusing events. Social work students might use journals for role-playing exercises to understand their client's situation. The journal can become the first articulation for any idea or experiment.

## Journals Across the Curriculum

When I began teaching in 1967, I sometimes assigned journals in composition and literature classes, but used them sparingly in the classroom itself, preferring to let students write on their own; some students used them well, while most never really understood what they were about. I no longer trust to chance. Journals work now for most students because we use them actively, every day to write in, read from, and talk about — in addition to whatever private writing the students do on their own. These everyday journal sessions take the place of other routine writing assignments from pop quizzes to homework and book reports. Journal writing in class stimulates student discussion, starts small group activity, clarifies hazy issues, reinforces learning experience and stimulates student imagination.

Journal writing works because every time students write, they individualize instruction; the act of silent writing, even for five minutes, generates ideas, observations, emotions. It is hard to daydream, doze off, or fidget while we write — unless we write about it. Journal writing will not make passive students miraculously active learners; however, regular writing makes it harder for students to remain passive.

At Michigan Technological University where I teach writing, the Humanities faculty coordinates a "writing across the curriculum" program to encourage teachers from every discipline to incorporate more writing in their classroom instruction. We conduct off-campus writing workshops which last from two to four days and introduce our colleagues, inductively, to a variety of ideas for using writing to enhance both learning and communication skills. Workshop topics include invention and brainstorming, rewriting and revision, editing, peer-response groups, evaluation, and journal writing.

We ask teachers of history, chemistry and business to keep a journal, themselves, for the duration of the workshop. Sometimes we start with a journal writing session asking participants, for example, to write down their opinion about the causes of poor student writing. Other times we ask the teachers to summarize or evaluate the worth of a particular workshop session by writing about it for five minutes in their journals. And still other times we ask them to "freewrite" in order to generate possible paper topics which will be expanded, later, into short papers. These five- and ten-minute writing exercises allow teachers to experience first-hand the potential of journal writing as an aid to learning.

Teachers who find value in journal writing at the faculty workshops often incorporate student journals into their subsequent classes. A professor of American history now uses journals as a regular part of his course in Michigan History. Periodically, he interrupts his lectures to ask students to write for a few minutes on a particular lecture point. In discussing the railroad system of the state, for example, he asks students to write for five minutes about their knowledge of trains — whether from personal experience, movies or books. He uses this brief writing time to engage his students more personally with the topic of his lecture. Later in the term, he will base an exam question on the mid-term or final on one of the in-class journal sessions.

A geography professor uses journals in two large lectures classes. In Recreational Geography, he asks students to keep journals to stimulate their powers of observation. By requiring students to write down what they see in their journals, he finds that they look more closely and carefully and, hence, begin to acquire the rudimentary techniques of scientific observation. He also requires students in Conservation to keep journals; specifically, at the beginning of new course topics, he asks them to write definitions of terms or concepts which they misuse or misunderstand. At the conclusion of each topic he requests another written definition to discover how their initial perceptions have changed. During the final week of the ten-week course, he asks students to compose an essay about their attitude changes toward conservation as a result of the course; the journal is the primary resource for this last assignment.

A political science professor who has been skeptical of journals throughout most of his twenty years of teaching has begun using journals in his course on American Government and Politics. He asks students to record frequently their opinions about current events in the journals; he also requests students to write short personal summaries of articles in their journals, thereby creating a sequential critical record of readings accomplished during the term. While both of these activities may be conducted through other written forms, using the bound journal is simple and economical.

A teacher of music asks her students to keep "listening journals" in which they record their daily experience of hearing music. Periodically, she conducts discussion classes which rely heavily on the subjective content of the journals, and so involves the students both personally and critically in her course content. In similar fashion, a drama teacher asks his actors to keep a journal to develop more fully their awareness of a character or scene in a play. He has found that his student actors write their way into their characters by using journals.

Professors in the technical curriculum have also found uses for journals. One metallurgy professor has prepared a full-page handout with suggestions to students about using journals in Introduction to Materials Science. He uses journals to encourage thoughtful reflection upon important topics, practice writing answers to possible exam questions, and improve writing fluency. More specifically, he asks students to write about each day's lecture topic prior to attending class; after class, they are asked to write a class summary or questions about the lecture. Periodically, these journals are checked to monitor student progress; they are not graded. In reading his first batch of one hundred journals he was surprised to discover few charts, diagrams or drawings among the student writing. As a consequence he has introduced a section on "visual thinking" into his course, as he believes that metallurgical engineers must develop visualization to a high degree. The journal was useful as it indicated the thinking processes of his students and so changed a part of his pedagogical approach.

In my own literature and composition classes I use journals daily. I may ask students to define "romanticism" in their own words, for five minutes, before talking about American romantic authors Emerson, Thoreau, or Whitman. Sometimes I stop a class early and ask for a few minutes of journal writing to allow students to reflect on the class discussion just completed. I assign journal writing as homework to prep students for the next class discussion: "How would you react if you were a Harvard divinity student and you just heard Emerson's 'Divinity School Address'?" These short exercises engage students directly with the material being read. Sometimes, when a poem or story is particularly difficult, I will ask students to write about the line or passage which they do *not* understand, for example "Write out in your words the meaning of 'Do not go gentle into that good night' or 'What if a much of a which of a wind'." By next class, students who have taken this suggestion seriously will have written themselves toward understanding.

So far I have talked about the journal as a pedagogical catalyst; an equally valuable function focuses student attention on language use. By reading passages out loud, or reproducing passages to share with the class, students become more conscious how their language affects people. Students in my freshman humanities class actually suggested that duplicated journal passages should become a part of the "humanistic" content of the course; we mimeographed selected journal entries, shared them for a week, and all learned more about each other. Passing journal entries around class suggested new writing possibilities to students; in this case, the stimulus to experiment came from classmates rather than teacher and so had the validity of peer education.

I am not concerned with *what* students write in their journals, nor even if they respond to all my suggestions. One student felt she wasn't doing the journal "correctly" because she kept drifting off into personal reflections — writing about her own religious convictions instead of, for example, role-playing an imaginary Harvard divinity student, as I had requested. What could I say? She made the material her own in the most useful way possible. I suspect that the best journals deviate far and freely from the questions I pose. In some disciplines, line electrical engineering or physics, homework questions might be less open-ended than those in liberal arts courses, but even in the most specialized fields some free, imaginative speculation helps. And when that speculation is recorded in the journal, students have a record to look at, later, to show where they have been and perhaps suggest where to go next.

Teachers find it easy to add more writing to a class by using journals. Regardless of class size, informal writing need not take more teacher-time; journals can be spot-checked, skimmed, read thoroughly, or not read at all, depending on the teacher's time, interest and purpose. Journals have proved to be remarkably flexible documents; some teachers call them *logs*, others *commonplace books*, still others *writers' notebooks*. While I prefer students to keep looseleaf binders, science teachers who are conscious of patient rights often require bound notebooks. While I suggest pens (pencils smear), a forestry teacher I know suggests pencils (ink smears in the rain). And so on. Individual permutations appear to be infinite.

## Academic Journals

What does a journal look like? How often should people write in them? What kinds of writing should they do on their own? How should I grade them? These questions often occur to the teacher who has not used or kept journals before. Here are some possible answers.

I describe journals to my class by explaining that journals exist somewhere on a continuum between diaries and class notebooks: whereas diaries are records of personal thought and experience, class notebooks are records of other people's facts and ideas. Like the diary, the journal is written in the first person; like the class notebook, the journal focuses on academic subjects the writer would like to learn more about. Journals may be focused narrowly, on the content of one discipline, or broadly, on the whole range of a person's experience. Each journal entry is a deliberate exercise in expansion: "How accurately can I describe or explain this idea? How far can I take it?" The journal demands the students expand their awareness of what is happening, personally and academically, to them.

Student writers should be encouraged to experiment with their journals, to write often and regularly on a wide variety of topics, to take some risks with form, style and voice. Students should notice how writing in the early morning differs from writing late at night. They might also experience how writing at the same time every day, regardless of mood, produces surprising results. Dorothy Lambert relaxes students by suggesting that "a journal is a place to fail. That is, a place to try, experiment, test one's wings. For the moment, judgment, criticism, evaluation are suspended; what matters is the attempt, not the success of the attempt."[7] She asks students to pay attention to writing as a process and quit worrying about product perfection — in this case, spelling, grammar, punctuation, form, diction, and style. For better or worse, the journal is the student's own voice; the student must know this and the teacher must respect it.

Peter Elbow urges students to engage in the process of discovery through "free writing," a technique that encourages writers to free associate while writing as fast as they can. Elbow writes: "You don't have to think hard or prepare or be in the mood: without stopping, just write whatever words come out — whether or not you are thinking or in the mood."[8] This process illustrates immediately, for most writers, the close relationship between writing and thinking. The journal is a natural place to freewrite. Students can practice it on their own to get their mental gears moving toward a paper topic; teachers can assign free writing to brainstorm new research projects. Keeping these exercises in journals guarantees a written record of the ideas generated, which may prove useful during the term of study or, later, to document intellectual growth.

Some teachers insist on not reading student journals, arguing they have no right to pry in these private academic documents. They have a point. However, I believe for a number of reasons that teachers ought to look at students' journals. First, the students just beginning to keep journals, a reading by a teacher can help them expand their journals and make them more useful. Sometimes first journals have too many short entries; a teacher who notices this can suggest trying full-page exercises to allow the writers more space to practice developing ideas. Second, some students believe that if an academic production is not looked at by teachers it has no worth; while there is more of a problem here than reading journals, the teacher may decide at the outset that looking at the journals will add needed credibility to the assignment. Third, students feel that journals must "count for something" — as must every requirement in an academic setting. "If teachers don't look at these things how can they count 'em?"

One way to count a journal as a part of the student's grade is to count pages. I know a teacher who grades according to the quantity of writing a student does; one hundred pages equals an 'A'; seventy-five a 'B'; fifty a 'C'; etc. Other teachers attempt to grade on the quality of insight or evidence of personal growth. Still other teachers prefer a credit/no credit arrangement. To complete the requirements for the course the students must show evidence they have kept a journal; these teachers need only to see the journal pages for evidence of use and do not read the entries. But this last method precludes the *teacher* from learning through the student's writing.

To resolve this apparent paradox between the student's need for a private place to write and the benefit to both student and teacher from at least a limited public reading, I ask students to keep their journals in a looseleaf format with cardboard dividers to separate sections of the journal. This way, I look at sections dealing with my course, but not at the more personal sections. If portions of the student's commentary about a particular class would prove embarrassing, the looseleaf allows the student to delete that entry prior to my perusal.

Reading students' journals keeps teachers in touch with student frustrations, anxieties, problems, joys, excitements. Teachers, regardless of discipline, who understand the everyday realities of student life may be better teachers when they tailor assignments more precisely toward student needs. Reading student journals humanizes teachers.

### Personal Journals

A student's journal can be a documentary of both academic and personal growth, a record of evolving insight as well as the tool used to gain that insight. In classes which explore values, such as philosophy, sociology, and literature, the journal can be a vehicle to explore the writer's own belief system.[9] In like manner, writing classes may benefit from using the journal for self-discovery. In *On Righting Writing*, Robert Rennert reports using a journal for deliberate values-clarification purposes throughout the semester. He asks students to use journals to rank their values, to make lists of "important human qualities," and to write their own obituaries. He confronts students and makes them objectify, to some extent, their own biases through responses to topics such as "What I want my clothes to say about me." Rennert reports encouraging results from his journal-focused class: "Confronted with significant questions and problems, students moved off dead center and were stimulated to discover, through writing, knowledge about their values and attitudes."[10]

The journal is a natural format for self-examination. The teacher can initiate the process of suggesting journal writing on traditional value-clarification questions: What color clothes do you usually wear and why? If your house was on fire and you could only save one object, what would it be? If you had only two more days to live, how would you spend them? These questions, and dozens of variations, force the writers to examine their lives closely and to find words in order to do so.

In *Composition for Personal Growth*, Hawley, Simon, and Britton offer teachers suggestions for posing developmental problems for their students. Under the heading "Journal-Synthesizing Activities" Hawley lists a number of imaginary situations which require journal-writers to move outside their writing and experience it from a different perspective. In an exercise called "Time Capsule" students are given these directions: "Your journal is discovered one hundred years from now (or three hundred years ago). You, your other-time counterpart, find the journal. Write a description of the person and the way of life revealed in the journal."[11] Tasks such as these provide students with the means to witness their own progress and, as such, are useful concluding exercises in any class using journals.

Teachers who have not done so should try keeping a journal along with their students. Journals do not work for everyone; however, the experience of keeping one may be the only way to find out. Teachers, especially, can profit by the regular introspection and self-examination forced by the process of journal writing. The journal allows sequential planning within the context of one's course — its pages become a record of what has worked, what hasn't, and suggestions for what might work next time — either next class or next year. Teachers can use journals for lesson plans, practice exercises, and class evaluation. The journal may become a teaching workshop and a catalyst to generate new research ideas as well as a record of pedagogical growth.

Teachers should consider doing journal writing daily, in class, along with their students. Teachers who write with their students and read entries out loud in class lend credibility to the assignment and test the validity of the writing task. If the instructor has a hard time with a given topic, it provides insight into difficulties students may encounter and so makes for a better assignment next time.

The teacher-kept journal provides an easy means to evaluate each class session. The journal is not the only way to do this, of course, but it provides a handy place to keep these records, alongside the planning sessions and the in-class journal. "Why was that discussion on Walt Whitman so flat today? If I had waited longer, instead of answering my own question, others might have spoken and deflected some of the attention away from me." Jottings like this may help teachers understand better their own teaching process and sometimes result in insights about what should or shouldn't have been done. These evaluations also act as prefaces for the next planning session, pointing toward more structure or less. And when a class, for one reason or another, has been a complete failure, writing about it can be therapeutic. I can objectify what went wrong and so create the illusion, at least, of being able to control it the next time.

Journals are interdisciplinary and developmental by nature; it would be hard for writers who use their journals regularly and seriously not to witness their own growth. For teachers in most disciplines, however, the personal nature of journals may be of secondary importance — at least to the teacher — with the primary focus remaining the student's grasp of specialized knowledge. However, the importance of coupling personal with academic learning should not be overlooked; self-knowledge provides the motivation for whatever other knowledge an individual learns and absorbs. Without an understanding of who we are, we are not likely to understand fully why we study biology rather than forestry, literature rather than philosophy. In the end, all knowledge *is* related; the journal helps clarify the relationships.

**Notes:**

1. James Britton, Tony Burgess, Nancy Martin, Alex McLeod, and Harold Rosen, *The Development of Writing Abilities* (11-18) (London: Macmillan, 1975), pp. 88-105.

2. *Ibid.*, p. 197.

3. *Ibid.*, p. 165.

4. Janet Emig, *The Composing Process of Twelfth Graders* (Urbana, Illinois: NCTE English Research Report No. 13, 1971).

5. Emig, "Writing as a Mode of Learning," *College Composition and Communication* (May, 1977), p. 122.

6. Daniel N. Fader and Morton H. Shaevitz, *Hooked on Books* (New York: Berkley 1966), p. 26.

7. "What is a Journal" in Ken Macrorie, *Writing to be Read*, 2nd ed. (Rochelle Park, New Jersey: Hayden, 1976), p. 151.

8. Peter Elbow, *Writing Without Teachers* (New York: Oxford University Press, 1973), p. 9.

9. Teachers and counselors will find a thorough discussion of the possible therapeutic uses of personal journals in Ira Progoff's *At a Journal Workshop* (New York: Dialogue House Library, 1975).

10. Robert A. Rennert, "Values Clarification, Journals, and the Freshman Writing Course," in *On Righting Writing*, ed. Ouida H. Clapp (Urbana, Illinois: NCTE, 1975), p. 106.

11. Robert Hawley, Sidney Simon and D. D. Britton, *Composition for Personal Growth* (New York: Hart, 1973), p. 142.

# Time for Questions: Writing Across the Curriculum

*B*RYANT FILLION *found that writing was not used to foster learning, but his conclusions comes from work in Canadian schools. What do surveys of U.S. schools reveal?*

Sadly, the pattern Fillion found does seem to be representative of U.S. schools as well. The most extensive study of U.S. classrooms is John Goodlad's *A Place Called School.* Goodlad found that while many teachers claimed that the purpose of instruction was to develop intellectual abilities, their teaching practices did not match their goals. I'll quote from his chapter, "What Schools and Classrooms Teach":

> What the schools in our sample did not appear to be doing in these subjects was developing all of those qualities commonly listed under "intellectual development": the ability to think rationally, the ability to use, evaluate, and accumulate knowledge, a desire for further learning. Only *rarely* did we find evidence to suggest instruction likely to go much beyond mere possession of information to a level of understanding its implications and either applying it or exploring its possible applications.

In another survey, Arthur Applebee *(Writing in the Secondary School)*, found that the most common type of writing in mathematics, science and social studies classes was notetaking. And even writing assignments which seemed to push students beyond the recall of information probably did not. Applebee gives these examples:

> Select some phase of 20th century American literature and discuss it in a theme of 300-500 words. Turn in polished draft only. (Eleventh Grade English)

> Explain the ability of the Constitution to change with the times. (Eleventh Grade American History)

> Write a brief essay describing a building (or type of building) which
> best represents 20th century American culture. (Ninth Grade
> World History)

Applebee notes that these assignments "become reasonable
tasks only when they are interpreted by students as requests to
summarize material previously presented in lessons or texts." (74).

*What kind of writing should be done in the subject areas?*

A big question. Students should be encouraged to use what
James Britton calls "expressive language" to work through key
questions. Expressive language resembles speech (see examples in
the letters in Nancie Atwell's article and in the reading narratives in
my own article). We can see it at work in the following journal entry
where a student works toward an understanding of what the
humanities are:

> At first I thought about just human behavior but when I think of
> the humanities I think of English and that doesn't fit in. It seems
> that human creative expression or communication might be a good
> short definition. Because I consider photography, drawing, paint-
> ing, writing, building, and lots of other stuff to be creative expres-
> sion. Humanities has to be a very general topic; so the definition
> would also have to be general. When someone mentioned subjec-
> tive, I agreed with that a lot. I think that separates it pretty well
> with the sciences. Scientists all seem to be very objective people
> with objective purposes. (Quoted in Fulwiler and Young, *Language
> Connections*.)

The writer is using writing to think aloud, to work toward a definition. A teacher could respond to a journal like this by raising
questions: what does "creative" mean? what are the "subjective"
purposes of humanists? Isn't a writer like Lewis Thomas a
"humanist" too?

Writing can also be used to support the thinking processes that
are central in each discipline. I grew up with a biologist and I was
always made aware of how important careful observation was. The
famous biologist Louis Aggasiz began his biology classes by having
his students look at a fish — for three full days. Students should be
encouraged to use writing to hone their own capacity to observe.
The historian must interpret documents, and if the subject is recent,
conduct interviews. There are a number of inquiry texts which provide students with historical documents that a student might read

and write about — *As It Happened: A History of the United States* by Charles Sellars et al. is one of the best. Students can also compile oral histories involving interviews with people who experienced history. Studs Terkel's *The Good War* could be used as a model.

*Does a heavy reliance on the textbook limit the kinds of writing students do in the content areas?*

I think so. Textbooks clearly have a major part to play, but other kinds of reading may be more useful in eliciting interpretation, analysis, and evaluation. Part of the problem, especially in the social studies area, is that the edges of controversy are blunted; Frances Fitzgerald presents a chilling picture of this process in *America Revised*. And textbooks in all areas seem designed on a "transmission" model of learning, where information is passed on to the student.

Students in science classes could profit from reading essayists like Stephen Gould, Lewis Thomas, and Loren Eisley. Students in computer classes could enjoy Tracy Kidder's *Soul of a New Machine* and students in a biology class could learn a great deal about diseases from Berton Roueche's, *The Medical Detectives*. Students in history classes could read books like Barbara Tuchman's *Guns of August* to understand the origins of World War I or A.J.P. Taylor's controversial *Origins of the Second World War* to understand how the world stumbled into that war. The list could go on.

Books of this kind provide the challenge of sustained reading that textbooks (particularly those which have, in Jean Chall's words, been "dumbed down") do not. Because they probe more deeply into particular topics they lend themselves to interpretation more easily than textbooks. Most importantly, they provide a model of writing that includes a human voice. Too many textbooks provide a neutral voice; there is no contact with a writer. If the only kind of exposition students have read is the textbook, they will, I feel, try to write like textbooks when they attempt to analyze or present information. We all know the dreary result.

*Most school curriculum define areas of knowledge that must be covered. Can teachers still cover the prescribed material and do the reading (outside the text) and writing you suggest?*

This is the dilemma. How are we to define the objectives of our teaching? I feel that we often think about curriculum as *material* to be covered rather than as *processes of thought*. The Goodlad study suggests that schools are emphasizing coverage of factual material at the expense of developing skills in interpreting, analyzing, and applying information. But if schools are to emphasize these intellectual capacities, they may need to scale down the range of information students are to master.

After all, the teacher's job is not to cover but to uncover.

# Suggestions for Further Reading:
## Writing Across the Curriculum

Applebee, Arthur. *Contexts for Learning to Write* (Norwood, N.J.: ABLEX Publishing Corporation, 1984).

Applebee, Arthur. *Writing in the Secondary School: English and the Content Areas* (Urbana, Illinois: National Council of Teachers of English, 1981).

Barnes, Douglas. *From Communication to Curriculum* (Harmondsworth, England: Penguin Books, 1976).

Britton, James *et al. The Development of Writing Abilities 11-18* (London: Macmillan Educational, 1976).

Emig, Janet, "Writing as a Mode of Learning," in Janet Emig, *The Web of Meaning* (Montclair, N.J.: Boynton Cook Publishers, 1983).

*English Journal*, April, 1978. This issue is devoted to teaching scientific writing.

Fulwiler, Toby and Art Young, editors. *Language Connections: Writing and Reading Across the Curriculum* (Urbana, Illinois: National Council of Teachers of English, 1982).

Goodlad, John. *A Place Called School* (New York: McGraw-Hill, 1984). See especially Chapter 7, "What Schools and Classrooms Teach."

Mayher, John, Nancy Lester, and Gordon Pradl. *Learning to Writing/Writing to Learn* (Deansboro, N.Y.: Boynton/Cook, 1983).

Maimon, Elaine *et al. Writing in the Arts and Sciences* (Cambridge, Massachusetts: Winthrop Publishers, 1981).

Martin, Nancy *et al. Writing and Learning Across the Curriculum* (Deansboro, N.Y.: Boynton/Cook Publishers, 1976).

Medway, Peter. *Finding a Language: Autonomy and Learning in the School* (London: Writers and Readers Publishing Cooperative, 1980).

Sizer, Theodore. *Horace's Compromise: The Dilemma of the American High School* (Boston: Houghton Mifflin, 1984).

## APPENDIX I: The Grammar Questions

*Arguments about the place of grammar instruction often go awry because "grammar" has so many meanings. How can these various meanings be distinguished?*

Patrick Hartwell (see suggested reading) has identified five different meanings generally given to the word "grammar." In abbreviated form these are:

1. Grammar-in-the-head. Speakers of any language internalize the syntax of the language. The child of five has internalized most of the language's grammatical rules. This knowledge is almost entirely tacit — the user cannot articulate the grammatical rules they apply when they speak. For example, the child will know that we would say:

   > throe fat men AND NOT fat three men

   even though he or she had never thought about the rule for placing adjectives in a series. We are not "taught" this kind of grammar; we learn it, Chomsky would argue, because we are biologically predisposed to learn it.

2. Grammar-as-linguistic science. Linguists attempt to construct models of "grammar in the head." These models are necessarily complex and are not designed to "help" the language user. Attempts during the late 60's to teach watered-down versions of transformational grammar were generally unsuccessful and were mercifully abandoned.

3. School Grammar. This is the "grammar" derived from Latin grammars which is found in textbooks like the Warriner series. In fact, Charlton Laird has referred to school grammar as "the grammar of Latin ingeniously warped to suggest English." Some of the definitions in school grammar are ridiculed by linguists as hopelessly fuzzy. School grammar texts inform students that "A sentence expresses a complete thought" and then later that a paragraph has "one main idea" and that an essay has "one point." Linguists recoil at this imprecision. But school grammars do not really claim to be scientifically precise — only generally useful.

4. Grammar-as-etiquette. Written language has certain conventions, and when writers (or speakers) deviate from these conventions, they use "bad grammar." Writing instruction in this century has been driven by an almost neurotic concern for this problem, but the argument that we should be concerned only with meaning (and not with mechanics) is equally misleading. Errors do matter. Mina Shaughnessy writes:

> Errors . . . are unintentional and unprofitable intrusions upon the consciousness of the reader. They introduce in accidental ways alternative forms in spots where usage has stabilized a particular form. . . . They demand energy without giving any return in meaning. They shift the reader's attention from where he is going (meaning) to how he is getting there (code). (*Errors and Expectations*, p. 12.)

The reader, after all, is "a buyer in a buyer's market."

5. Grammar-as-style. There are a number of books which stress the conscious manipulation of sentences in order to help students become aware of stylistic options. Some of these presuppose that the writer understands school grammar (see Christensen); other proponents of grammar-as-style (many of the sentence-combining texts) do not presuppose this knowledge..

These distinctions help clarify the debate about grammar. Grammar-in-the-head is something we possess as a member of our species. Grammar-as-linguistic science is essentially unteachable except at the high levels of education. The question usually comes down to: does school grammar improve grammar-as-etiquette?

*I've read statements which claim that research has proved the grammar instruction does not improve writing ability. If this is the case shouldn't grammar instruction be entirely eliminated from the curriculum?*

The most widely quoted statement about the ineffectiveness of grammar instruction comes from a 1963 publication *Research in Written Composition*. Based on a review of almost 70 years of research the authors claim:

> In view of the widespread agreement of research studies based on many types of students and teachers, the conclusion can be stated in strong and unqualified terms: the teaching of formal grammar has a negligible or, because it displaces some instruction and practice in composition, even a harmful effect on improvement in writing. (37-38)

Many have used this conclusion to claim that grammar should not be taught at all.

In the past few years, though, there has been some skepticism about this sweeping claim (see the Kolnn article cited in the bibliography). Many of the studies cited in the 1963 survey do not meet current standards for experimental control, many failed to define what "instruction in formal grammar" meant, and many came up with ambiguous results. It is fair to say, however, that formal grammar instruction, while it may not be as harmful as the 1963 survey claims, is clearly not as essential to writing instruction as many programs seem to suggest it is. There is *no* reason to place any student in a writing class where actual experience writing is limited so that formal grammar might be taught.

But many have difficulty accepting the sweeping claim for no grammar because at times grammatical knowledge seems useful. Take for example a student who writes:

> She came in like she always did. Taking her good sweet time.

I've always found it easier to explain the fragment error to a student, if that student could find the subject and verb in a sentence. Without that minimal formal sense of what constitutes a sentence, a student has, I feel, a much harder time determining the problem and the solution.

The problem with most grammar instruction is that it is not limited to the kinds of knowledge that might come in useful to the writer. I've never had occasion to use the distinction between transitive and intransitive verbs yet I can remember a string of teachers trying to beat that into my head.

*If you accept that this minimal grammar instruction might be useful, how should it be taught — in grammar units?*

It should be taught in small doses. I've found few things more tedious (for students and for teachers) than grammar units that last for a period of weeks. Beside the obvious motivational problems, there is the problem of transfer. Even those students who may learn grammatical principles in the unit will often not transfer this learning to their own writing.

If grammar is to be taught it should be taught in mini-lessons of 5-7 minutes at the beginning of some writing classes. The lesson should deal with an issue that relates to the writing that students are doing. If students are overusing particular descriptive words — or using words like "awesome" to describe just about anything — a mini-lesson could focus on finding substitutes for these overworked adjectives. By relating grammar instruction to actual writing problems, the instruction has a better chance of sticking.

*Why do students make grammatical errors?*

For many students writing is a slow process that strains the writer's memory. To get something of a feel for this slowness, try writing with your non-writing hand. Most people when asked to make this switch find it difficult to maintain the sense of what they write because so much of their attention is given over to letter formation. Under these conditions, it is easy to see how a writer may get lost within a sentence and how grammatical errors are sometimes caused by breakdowns in attention.

Writers also get lost when they try to convey complex meanings that require the use of subordinating constructions which the writer initially mismanages. For example, a sentence quoted in Mina Shaughnessy's *Errors and Expectations:*

> If he or she feels that they would prefer going to college to take a course and major in something that has any doubt about whether or not they will be employed in the field that they have chosen then they should. (61)

The thought behind this sentence is not simple. I would translate it as: A person going to college should be willing to take a course that may not lead to employment if he or she wants to. Shaughnessy argues that attempts to consolidate ideas in sentences like this "though the attempts lead to ungrammaticality, may show a responsiveness to the writing situation that should be encouraged and not checked by a permanent retreat into simple sentences. . . ." (51) Errors of this kind might be referred to as "developmental errors" not caused by carelessness but by an attempt to tackle complex grammatical structures.

*What can a teacher do when confronted by such convoluted sentences?*

A first step would be to have the student read the paper aloud; students who have difficulty writing often do not reread what they have written. Some of these difficulties may become apparent to the student when he hears the sentences aloud. An audience for the writing can also help the student re-enter the text. A student listening to the sentence about picking courses might ask: "Are you saying people should or shouldn't take courses that won't lead to jobs?" This might push the writer to reformulate the sentence — at first orally and then, perhaps, in a revision.

*Is there anything that can be done for high school students with spelling problems?*

Poor spellers often think that the problem is unmanageable. If they make 30 spelling errors in a 500 word paper, they often see these 30 errors as thirty distinct problems. In fact, most poor spellers spell the vast majority of the words they use correctly, and even their misspellings are usually off by no more than a letter or two. These misspellings often fall into 2 or 3 categories; for example, a student may frequently leave off the sound at the end of words because he or she doesn't hear it. One of the teacher's main jobs is to show the student a pattern in these errors so that the problem does not seem so hopeless.

Poor spellers, like students who make grammatical errors, often do not reread what they have written. Students should be asked to read aloud their writing and to note words they are not sure of. Most adults, I believe, correct their misspellings, not by applying a rule, but by seeing if the word "looks right" — we match the word against some visual representation of that word. If the student has located a word that seems misspelled he should note the *part of the word* that seems questionable. The student can then look the word up.

If students are to master spelling lists, the words should be taken from their own misspellings. Standardized spelling lists seem less useful because students usually know how to spell most of the words on them. Why use valuable time testing students on words they already know? And the fact that a student has used a word is some indication that he or she will use it again. It makes more sense to concentrate on these words than to ask students to learn to spell words that they will not likely use.

*Are some spelling problems really handwriting problems?*

I think so. Some students write so illegibly that it may be difficult for many of them to clearly *see* the words they have written. These students should be given access to word processors, if they are available. The screen of the word processor will give them a clearer picture of what they have written — and it will give them a way of correcting misspellings that won't require constant smudgy erasing.

# Suggestions for Further Reading:
## The Grammar Question

Christensen, Francis. *Notes Toward a New Rhetoric; Nine Essays for Teachers* revised edition (New York: Harper and Row, 1978).

D'Eloia, Sarah. "The Uses — and Limits — of Grammar," *Journal of Basic Writing*, 1 (Spring/Summer, 1977), 1-20.

Daiker, Donald, Andrew Kerek, and Max Morenberg. *The Writer's Options: Combining to Composing* second edition (New York: Harper and Row, 1982).

DeBeaugrand, Robert. "Forward to the Basics: Getting Down to Grammar," *College Composition and Communication*, 35 (October, 1984), 358-367.

Elley, W. B., H. Lamb, and M. Wyllie. "The Role of Grammar in a Secondary School English Curriculum," *Research in the Teaching of English* 10 (1976): 5-21.

Hairston, Maxine. "Not All Errors Are Created Equal: Non Academic Readers Respond to Lapses in Usage," *College Composition and Communication*, 43 (December, 1981): 794-806.

Hartwell, Patrick. "Grammar, Grammars and the Teaching of Grammar," *College English*, 47:4 (February, 1985): 105-127.

Kolnn, Martha. "Closing the Books on Alchemy," *College Composition and Communication*, 32 (May, 1981): 139-151.

Moffett, James. "Grammar and the Sentence" in his *Teaching the Universe of Discourse* (Boston: Houghton Mifflin, 1983).

Shaughnessy, Mina. *Errors and Expectations* (New York: Oxford University Press, 1977).

Williams, Joseph. "The Phenomenology of Error," *College Composition and Communication* 32 (May, 1981): 152-168.